7/13

D1211509

HOT DOUG'S

The Sausage Superstore

773-279-9550

HOT DOUG'S
The Book

Doug Sohn WITH Kate DeVivo

MIDWAY

AN AGATE IMPRINT

CHICAGO

Design by Brandtner Design.

Printed in China.

Hot Doug's: The Book
By Doug Sohn with Kate DeVivo

First Printing June 2013
Hardcover ISBN: 978-1-57284-137-6
Ebook ISBN: 978-1-57284-720-0

Library of Congress Cataloging-in-Publication Data is on file at the Library of Congress.

10 9 8 7 6 5 4 3 2 1

Midway is an imprint of Agate Publishing, Inc. Agate books are available in bulk at discount prices.
For more information visit agatepublishing.com.

To B.L.T.

Table of Contents

Foreword BY GRAHAM ELLIOT

Seven words: "The Sausage Superstore and Encased Meat Emporium." It would be nice to say that this tag line adequately describes Hot Doug's, but it doesn't even come close. The name itself, Hot Doug's, tells you that chef and proprietor Doug Sohn is not only dedicated to the art of the hot dog, but he also has an irreverent sense of humor. Luckily for all of us, that humor shines through in his unsurpassed gastronomic creations.

Be it restaurants, casual eateries, or catering companies, Chicago offers a plethora of places to work in the food and beverage trade. As a graduate of the prestigious Kendall College, Doug's culinary opportunities were virtually limitless. Yet even though there were easier paths to take, with his entrepreneurial spirit burning like a grill on the Fourth of July, he tossed aside the idea of working for someone else's dream and made his own dream come true.

Now, I can tell you from personal experience, the decision to follow the beat of your own drummer is a double-edged sword. On one hand you can be yourself, answer to nobody, and stick it to the man! On the other hand, if things go wrong, you have nobody to blame but yourself. It's all part of The American Dream.

As Doug now enters his second decade of being the "top dog" in the hot dog world—having satisfied the hunger of many thousands of happy, cultish customers and having been awarded countless accolades and awards—it's safe to say that he made the right decision to follow his gut.

What's even more amazing is that in this current world of "celebrity chefs," restaurateurs generally jump at the chance to expand their "brand" and exploit their success. Not this guy; he believes that if your name is on the door you have a personal responsibility to be there for your customers.

Doug has now taken this a step further by creating this truly unique book. It's as if a superb magician has decided to share his secrets with us, letting us enjoy his stories and creativity. But like the restaurant, his customers have helped him create a unique experience with this book. The stories inside these pages are not only from Doug, but also from more than 225 loyal visitors and fans who have written memories, shared photos, and helped tell the Hot Doug's success story.

OK, so here's the part where I give you a quick history lesson on the romantic relationship of Chicago and the hot dog. These two lovebirds first met back at the 1893 World's Columbian Exposition. After seeing each other off and on for a few decades, things got hot and heavy during the Great Depression. Street vendors located on fabled Maxwell Street offered up dogs for a nickel, thus satisfying both the palates and wallets of the common working man.

It was at this time that the hot dog made its move and proposed to the city, consummated their love, and settled down to live happily ever after. The result: the true Chicago Dog, which, for the record, consists of chopped onion, a pickle spear, tomatoes, neon relish, mustard, pickled peppers, and celery salt, all on a poppy seed bun. Please note: any mention of the word ketchup and you're likely to get some squirted on you. Don't say I didn't warn you.

As with any great institution, every once in a while, when the planets are aligned and the gods are feeling generous, a visionary comes along and completely rewrites the rules. Ladies and gentlemen, I'm here to tell you that Doug Sohn is one of these visionaries. Monday through Saturday, between the hours of 10:30 a.m. and 4:00 p.m.—not a minute earlier or later—Hot Doug's provides the masses with the most delectable treats ever stuffed inside buns, to say nothing of his amazing duck-fat fries.

And when I say masses, I mean people literally lined up in a queue that wraps around the building, as if they were waiting for tickets to the latest Oscar-winning movie. I know from personal experience as I've been among these people, secretly hoping that Doug would see me and let me cut to the front. This has yet to happen.

With a DIY ethos that permeates the restaurant, it wouldn't be far off to say that Hot Doug's serves up edible punk rock. Reinventing the classics with humor, using ingredients such as rattlesnake and alligator not as a gimmick but as a way to show off their deliciousness or using foie gras in the face of the city's ridiculous ban—all of these cement the fact that Doug Sohn follows the beat of his own drum.

This book is filled with soul. Like the layers of an onion, each page reveals further insight about the artist that is Hot Doug and the experience that is Hot Doug's. Iconoclast, trailblazer, chef, Abe Froman, "The Sausage King of Chicago," entrepreneur, all-around ninja badass; you can call him what you want, but by the end of this book, you'll be calling him "friend."

....

Graham Elliot is a critically acclaimed chef, restaurateur, and television personality, and one of the most recognized faces cooking in America today. At age 27, he became the youngest Four Star Chef to be named in any major US city and was named one of Food & Wine *Magazine's "Best New Chefs." In addition to owning his three restaurants, including the eponymous restaurant that hold two Michelin stars, Graham is a judge on Fox's* MasterChef *and the culinary director of the Lollapalooza music festival.*

Introduction

This book wasn't my idea. I never had any intention to do this. Not only that, I had resisted more than one offer to write a book. Why? (1) It seemed like a lot of work. (2) I had really no idea how to create a book out of the restaurant. (3) It would legitimize the restaurant.

Now, I know intellectually that last one makes absolutely no sense to you. But it makes perfect sense to me. No joke—I still kind of consider Hot Doug's a pop-up restaurant, some sort of sham that people will finally realize is a hoax. And while this sounds like I may have some issues (and I'm not totally denying that), it's generally how I feel each day behind the counter. Not that Hot Doug's is like a dream, but...the success and kudos remain totally beyond my comprehension. Publishing a book would, to me, set this all in concrete.

So when my dear friend Kate DeVivo started talking to me about doing a book, and making me go to meetings about doing a book, I immediately got somewhat defensive. It took a few more meetings, a fair amount of cajoling, and a lot of convincing until I finally relented, with the proviso that the three most important words will be "as told to." I think I got a little ripped off on that one.

As the ideas for the book started forming, I realized quickly that this was going to be something I actually should do, if for no other reason than it would be nice to actually remember some of the history and get it down on paper before it totally disappears. I also came to the conclusion, being as objective as possible, that there may be kind of an interesting story here.

I also wanted a place for our customers to tell their stories. I am so overwhelmed by the outpouring of contributions and incredibly flattering words. It's the one part of Hot Doug's that I truly

have no experience with. To be perfectly honest, it's always perturbed me ever so slightly that the one person who would love this restaurant the most (They only serve sausage? They play the Ramones? The guy tells really old jokes?) is the one person who couldn't eat here, at least not without worrying too much about what else was going on. (Me.)

Kate and I had a great time working on this book. It brought back a lot of great memories, not to mention it was pretty fun sitting at a desk and just writing. I also got to go out for lunch. I enjoyed that, too. — **Doug Sohn**

A NOTE FROM THE EDITOR

Once Doug decided to do a book, I had the task of helping him figure out what it should be while making it as little work as possible for him. Thanks to my husband, Matt Green, who knows the uses of social media much better than Doug and me (and who also supports the notion of doing as little as possible), we settled on a concept one night when we were all out to dinner: ask Hot Doug's customers to help us write the book by sending us their stories through Facebook, Twitter, and email. After a few glasses of wine, it seemed genius—Matt and Doug's social media guy, Brendan Fitzpatrick, would help us come up with and post questions, and we would sit back and watch the stories come in.

It became clear right away that not only were we going to get far more stories than we could ever put in the book, but there are so many ways to tell the Hot Doug's story. While Hot Doug's the place is Doug Sohn's concept, Hot Doug's the experience is what happens beyond the sausages. It's where families meet once a year and talk for an hour because there's nothing else to do when you're standing in line. It's where friends celebrate birthdays, couples get engaged, new parents take their babies, and girlfriends go when they ditch work. It's where local politicians, musicians, lawyers, actors, and foodies of all ages go when they want some really good food at a decent price—and to have a good time.

Hot Doug's: The Book is meant to be a compilation of all of these things—Doug's memories, customer stories, and hopefully a good time for the reader. I knew I would have a great time working with Doug on this book—I can't thank him enough for this opportunity, which made my day-to-day job so much fun for the last year or so. I also thoroughly enjoyed working with all 250 of our other coauthors on this book. The contributors were all genuinely kind, helpful, and fun throughout all exchanges I had with them. After working on this book, I not only have a better sense of what makes Hot Doug's so special, but I know exactly why Doug enjoys his job so much. — **Kate DeVivo**

The Concept

CHAPTER 1

How One Question Led to a Restaurant

Can You Make a Bad Hot Dog?

When I worked as a cookbook editor at a Chicago-area publishing company, I would spend roughly one hour a day chatting with my friend and colleague, Paul Kelly. I still managed to get my work done, as evidenced by the *Campbell's Soup*, *Simple Grilling*, and *Slow Cooker* cookbooks that dominate the half-off shelves at your local big box and/or outlet stores. Our conversations would normally fall into one of three categories: (1) sports, (2) pop culture (although I'd have to explain pretty much all of it to him), and (3) inane questions. (An example: If you had to eliminate one state, which one would you choose? I think we decided on Indiana due to lack of interesting local food, and because it's a suburb of Chicago, although West Virginia may have been close. Of course, if you are reading this book right now and happen to live in Indiana, we were just kidding—West Virginia was the clear winner.) One Monday, during the course of our normal chat time, Paul mentioned he'd eaten a bad hot dog at lunch. This sparked the inane question that started it all: Is it possible to make a bad hot dog?

Hours of discussing this matter led to regular biweekly lunches, each time at a different local hot dog stand. Joining us were two other colleagues, Leah Yarrow and Cara Grady—although when Cara left the company, Jill Oldham took her place as a junior member of the group; the "junior" part she is still, to this day, bitter about. Everyone was required to get a hot dog, fries, and a soda, and after lunch we would write and discuss our reviews. Over the course of two years, the four of us, plus several guests, ended up going to more than 40 different Chicagoland restaurants. We discovered something interesting: While the Chicago-style hot dog has a good reputation, there were very few places doing it right. In fact, the hot dog was rarely the main focus of these establishments—they had other things, like burgers, chicken sandwiches, and pizza puffs. As we continued with the Hot Dog Club, the reviews would get longer and more detailed, and include more than just the food—we rated the ambience, the service, and so on. The Hot Dog Report grew to be several pages that recounted not only our thoughts on the food, but also anything that happened at lunch that day.

BEST/WORST DECISIONS

BEST DECISION:
Not calling the restaurant "Schleppy's, the Bulvan"

WORST DECISION:
Opening six days a week instead of five

After several lunches I started to get a really good idea of what made a place work: a good menu and a well-run shop. I also knew which places were just a mess, and I started thinking about how they could tweak this a little bit here or there to improve. I realized that a restaurant is like any other retail establishment—to be done right, it must offer quality goods for a fair value, and proper customer service. Then an idea started forming in my head.

A SCHLEPPY IS BORN BY PAUL KELLY

After lunch one day, I waltzed into my coworker's quirkily decorated cubicle. Doug at the time was a cookbook editor, and I worked for the same publishing company. I wanted Doug's take on how someone could screw up a hot dog.

I had gone to a hot dog stand in Lincolnwood. The hot dog was cold, not really cooked, on a soggy bun. It was dressed with too much relish and not enough yellow mustard or onions. There was no celery salt added. One single, lonely, sad excuse for a sport pepper sat forlornly on the end of the bun.

"How can you screw up a hot dog?" I asked Mr. Sohn. "It should be the easiest thing in the world to make correctly."

"Oh, no, my friend," Doug replied. "I would venture to guess that it is hard to find a correctly made Chicago hot dog."

Thus began the long hard slog known as the Hot Dog Club. Our quest was to visit as many hot dog stands as we could in and around Lincolnwood, a Northwest suburb of Chicago where our office was located.

We picked up one member, Leah, who suggested we go to Big Herm's in Skokie. Shortly thereafter, Jill Oldham horned her way into the club, because she was not able to not be included in anything we were doing. Jill was not a full member; she was an auxiliary, because we are not nice friends. (That is, Doug and I aren't. Leah is very nice.)

So there it was. Our mission was to find the best Chicago-style hot dog on the Northwest side. We ordered the same hot dog (mine was "with everything") at each place. We then set about grading the joints on their respective hot dog, fries, drink, atmosphere, customer service, and so on. We went to about 40 or 50 places. My cardiologist was overjoyed.

During these forays, we needed something to amuse ourselves other than the general pickiness with which we would eye the hot dog stand. Since I was the goy toy of the trio-plus-Jill, the other two, along with Jill, were chosen to educate me with the Yiddish Word of the Day.

Oh, we had many Yiddish words, some of which I had heard before and kind of knew what they meant—mashugana or schlep—and several I had never heard before: mensch, macher, bashert, bulvan. It was my task to try to come up with a definition of the word, and to use it in a sentence. Come on, I grew up in a Catholic neighborhood in Cincinnati!

Bulvan. That's how this whole thing started. Bulvan. Having no idea how to spell it, I guessed that the definition of bulvan was: an idiot-savant whose talent was being a rodeo clown. And my sentence went something like, "Schleppy had no other discernible skills in life, but as a rodeo clown he had a singular talent for keeping bucking bulls off of fallen cowboys. He was a real bull-vant." At least that's how I guessed it was spelled.

Anyway, Schleppy went from "bull-vant" to mascot of the fictional hot dog joint we were going to open called Schleppy's. We jokingly imagined how the place would be run. Little did any of us realize that all Doug wanted to be in life was Schleppy.

All in all...it's pretty close to an "A"...if only it served beer!

THIS, MY FRIENDS, IS HOW IT BEGAN BY LEAH YARROW

I get all verklempt when I reminisce about the Hot Dog Club. I do not use that word—verklempt—lightly. First of all, being in the Hot Dog Club was the most creative, entertaining, and delicious highlight of my work life. Second of all, it's a well-known Yiddish word so we didn't need to teach it to Paul or include it in our Char Yiddish Dictionary.

The reviews! The lunchtime revelry continued when we returned to our cubicles and wrote our critiques. We covered dog, bun, fixings, fries, drink, counter help, décor, ambience, the parking lot, and each other. And we'd have to use the Yiddish Word of the Day in the reviews. Some words, like geshmak (tasty), were easy to incorporate into the write-ups; others, like pupik (belly button), were more difficult. We hungered for a challenge!

Although we were serious and merciless critics, we also focused on cracking each other up. We waited impatiently for the reviews to come in. Doug kept track of delinquent reviewers, and also compiled the reviews and developed a sophisticated system of averaging grades (though it could have been completely arbitrary since we have no idea how he did it). Those of us who sat near each other could hear chuckling and even snorts of laughter as we read each other's comments. Sometimes we'd just have to get up and visit for a minute after reading to reprise the jokes.

For the Hot Dog Club, funny was as important as the frankfurter—and on many occasions comic relief saved a particularly unpleasant dogging: the cold hot dogs, frigid indoor temperatures, soggy buns, surly counter help, wrong orders, the wearing of cheese fries delivered by a sudden gust of wind when we ate outdoors, a disgusting drum of grease. But nothing was worse than the horror (and shandeh) of receiving a hot dog buried in, or even just gilded with, ketchup. Though that gave us something to mock later.

Although we all agreed in theory on what constituted a great Chicago hot dog (and fries), we rarely agreed on a grade for a particular establishment. A stale bun and snapless dog for one of us could be a perfectly charred sausage in a properly steamed and seeded bun for another.

That's why we began to fantasize about opening our own hot doggery. Well, that and because there was no place that got everything right and so many that got almost everything wrong. We dreamed up new items to offer alongside the best hot dog in town. My contribution: a matzo ball on a stick. Needless to say, that's not on the Hot Doug's menu. Perhaps if it were encased in sausage?

But that's all hot dogs under the bridge (I think we ate there once). Doug has created a greater hot dog club, a sausage-loving community with unlimited membership. There is no finer hot dog establishment this side of paradise. AAA+++.

Kvell (to be proud)!

REFLECTIONS OF A HOT DOG CLUB MEMBER OF JUNIOR STANDING BY JILL YOUNGMANN OLDHAM

When Doug asked me to contribute to this book, I was thrilled. Little old me, a junior associate member of the Hot Dog Club? My thoughts, printed in blue and white, right next to the likes of Paul Kelly (yes, that Paul Kelly, soaked in beer and proud of it) and Leah Yarrow, founding members in full standing? Aw, shucks!

My next reaction? Doggonit! Those days, so long ago, are shrouded in a hot dog haze. But it wasn't long before I was on a roll, attacking this assignment with relish. (I know, I know, groan.) Puns like that were the name of the game in those days, when we would gaily head out at lunchtime to the hot dog venue du jour; order a dog, fries, and a soda; teach the Swinging Gentile a new Yiddish word; eat, drink, and be merry; and then dutifully and thoughtfully type up a review. Did the dog have the right amount of flavor and snap? Were the tomatoes fresh? Was the bun soggy? Were the fries hand-cut or—oy, gevalt—frozen?

We were harsh critics, to be sure, and many were the excursions in which the company and banter far outshone the fare. Soon Doug was compiling our reviews into a poor man's "newsletter," and our opinions were made public for all who cared—and let's be honest, no one cared but us. Doug cared the most, and with each outing and report, a poppy seed of an idea began to take hold. For every A grade, there were more than a few Bs and Cs, and the A-pluses were few and far between. Surely, he speculated, he could do better than the majority of these joints! I speak for the Hot Dog Club (though I am but a lowly junior associate member) when I say yes, yes he could. And he certainly did.

So am I disappointed I never made it past junior associate status before the club disbanded? Hell yes. But does the success of Hot Doug's wiener stand help ease that pain? Well, no, not in the middle of winter when I'm standing in line half a block away from the front door, wondering bitterly if Leah and Paul, as full-fledged members, are allowed to bypass the line. But when I'm enjoying duck fat fries and a perfectly char-grilled dog (pickle, tomato, and sauerkraut only, NO MUSTARD), hot diggity dog, it sure does.

A+.

DOGGERY	DOUG	LEAH	PAUL The Swinging Gentile	JILL
ANONYMOUS DOGGERY 1 CUMULATIVE GRADE: # B	**GRADE: B** Not a bad doggie. Worth the ride? Probably not. No flaying of the dog, I like that. Tasty condiments. A properly steamed bun. The fries could have been hotter and saltier, although I thoroughly enjoyed the Cheez Whiz poured on top of the "cheddar" fries. Excellent service.	**GRADE: A-** A very, very good dog. Perfectly grilled, with snap, plenty of fixings, and a decent bun. An abundance of mediocre fries. And there was the thrill of making some Northbrook moms uncomfortable enough to give us their table.	**GRADE: C** The fixins are important to a Chicago dog. I want to taste each ingredient yet have them work together in a symphony of flavor. Granted, it's the first day of December, but the tomato was mushy. The celery salt and onions were virtually nonexistent, and thus the mustard and relish dominated. I did get sport peppers, however, and the dog itself was tasty, but the fries could use a little work.	**GRADE: B/B+** I think I was swayed by all the preliminary positive publicity. While the dog was good, it did not achieve greatness. Was it tasty? Yes. Did it have snap? A little bit. Was it extraordinary? I'm sorry, I don't think so. Fries were decent, although the cheddar was a bit bland. I like a little bit of attitude from the staff, so that was good. To sum it up: not worth the commute, but a fine choice for when I'm in the neighborhood.

DOGGERY	DOUG	LEAH
ANONYMOUS DOGGERY 2 CUMULATIVE GRADE: # A+	**GRADE: A+** From the bottom of their pure-beef heart, this place makes one damn fine dog. Big, loads of snap, finely charred, good condiments (especially the pickle). The bun gets a little less soggy because it is lounging contentedly cushioned inside its trademarked box, but it's fresh and seeded. The crinkle-cut fries were perfectly cooked and seasoned—finally a doggery that keeps its saltshaker near the deep fryer. And the Coke was excellent—the right size, proper ice-to-soda ratio, syrup proportional. Even though we didn't get to eat in the car, this doggery receives no flanken grade, that's for sure.	**GRADE: A++** There just ain't no dogging like this place. And I can say this with certainty after—gasp!—39 trips to doggeries. This dog is superb. No scrawny excuse for a wiener, this dog is substantial. It has bite and snap and flavor and some char, I think. We waited (a bit too) long for it. (Hey, this ain't no flanken.) Two pickles of deli quality, and a green tomato: bliss. Perfect crinkle fries. OK, they didn't serve us in "the manner that will make you want to return" (a little surly on the counter help), but you can forgive them for thinking all customers are familiar with their routine.

NOTE FROM DOUG:

THE SNAP IS KEY. "SNAP" IS THE ONOMATOPOEIA THAT RESULTS FROM BITING INTO A NATURAL CASING WIENER. IT'S MOSTLY A TEXTURAL SENSATION, BUT I THINK IT AFFECTS THE FLAVOR AS WELL. IT GIVES THE HOT DOG A CRISPY AND CRACKLY OUTER TEXTURE, AND NOT A MUSHY ONE THAT YOU OFTEN GET FROM UNCASED WIENERS.

...JL (...winging Gentile) | **JILL**

GRADE: A

...archbishop
...ad this dog,
...uld have
...special
...nsation for
...as well. I may
...ing to hell for
...g non-corned
...meat on Friday
...g Lent, but
...ast the dog
...worth it. The
...age was nicely
...red and filled
...spices. (What's
...eal with that?
...do these hot
...s taste like
...e are spices
...em when they
...supposedly
...same Vienna
...sages?) The
...s were great
...perfectly
...ortionate (thus
...inating the
...a "+" and the
...o-hip-hooray,"
...ause I like my
...s over the top).
...e bun. Great
...s. Because it's
...Patty's day, a
...erick: There was
...ot dog stand
...st of Lincoln,
...t was somewhat
...se to Sohn's kin.
...d tho' I shoulda
...d grouper, the
...g there was
...per, made with
...kinda beef, even
...nken.

GRADE: A

That was one super dog. First of all, it was huge. Secondly, what a great char. Steamed bun; yummy green tomato; tasty fries… no complaints whatsoever. I love this dog. I offer up my apologies to the crew for being the wet blanket who insisted we eat inside. My membership in the Hot Dog Club has come to an end for now, but I take comfort in knowing that everything has an end—except the sausage, which has two. I'll hold the memory of this wonderful dogging experience close to my heart until the next time I'm able to dog with you guys.

DOGGERY	DOUG	LEAH	PAUL (The Swinging Gentile)	JILL
ANONYMOUS DOGGERY 3 CUMULATIVE GRADE: # C+	GRADE: B A nice dog with good condiments, although the bun was not quite up to snuff (a tad dry and not steamed, the way I like it). Excellent fries come gratis with said doggie, and nobody likes the serve-yourself sodas like I do. The service gets a big round of applause! I would like to confirm that the necessity of taking a two-hour nap immediately after eating a char dog isn't merely a bubbiemeiser.	GRADE: A- (dog) D (comfort) Despite the chopped sport peppers' attempt to imitate relish (a shaneh gelechter), they were a brilliant addition to a very snappy, well-charred, well-seasoned dog. Usually you have to chase sport peppers and keep tucking them back into the bun, and you end up with no pepper in some bites and too much in others. But not with these chopped ones. You got a taste of pepper in every bite. Good-sized dog, good bun. And the fries were crisp and nice and greasy like I like 'em. Personally, I would have rather eaten in a minivan (or two) because there would have been much more room.	GRADE: D+ OK. No more Mr. Nice Mensch. You know what? The bun was terribly stale, the pickle was limp, and "everything" was missing tomatoes, onions, and celery salt (well, I didn't taste the celery salt, at least). Why not an F? Because the chopped sport peppers were a tasty and unexpected treat, and the fries were done correctly.	GRADE: C I really wanted to hate this dumpy, dingy place, but I couldn't. The dog was really pretty tasty, full of bite, and well charred (also quite intricately flayed). Fries were pretty good too, but neither dog nor fries were great enough to make up for the very yucky atmosphere. When I'm on a hot dog excursion, I'm sorry, but I'd like to take off my coat and sit at a booth or table with my esteemed colleagues to savor the experience. This place proved pretty miserable in that respect.

Thanks to these folks for their hand in my education about what's good and what what is not so good at hot dog stands:

ORIGINAL MEMBERS OF HOT DOG CLUB:
PAUL KELLY
LEAH YARROW
CARA GRADY
JILL OLDHAM

GUEST STARS:
AMANDA KELLY
LEX, THE WONDER DOG
NICK MARKOS
EVAN OLDHAM
KYLE OLDHAM
DARCY SMITH
BEN YARROW
NATHAN YARROW

At this juncture, I was sort of bored at my current job; I didn't really want to continue with what I was doing or take a promotion. I knew I needed something else. And I wanted to get back into food and be a little more hands-on, which I hadn't really done since just after culinary school. I was intrigued by the idea of a hot dog stand. As we did our weekly hot dog lunches, I kept thinking, could I do this? Is it plausible? I grew up in Chicago, loving hot dog stands and loving to eat hot dogs. And I knew there were these other types of sausages out there, but no one

YIDDISH WORD OF THE DAY
At some point during the Hot Dog Club era, Jill, Leah, and I started talking about Yiddish words, and we started incorporating the Yiddish Word of the Day for Paul, who ended up becoming "The Swinging Gentile" for some reason. We would always give Paul the word of the day, and ask him to use it in a sentence before he knew the definition. And we would try to incorporate the word into our reviews as well.

Top 10 Yiddish Words of the Day Used in the Hot Dog Report

1. **Bshert:** *meant to be ("It was bshert that Paul would pay for hot dogs today.")*

2. **Bulvan:** *an uncouth man; a brute with no sensitivity ("Many people consider Paul a bulvan. I think he's just drunk.")*

3. **Chazerai:** *junk (any kind, but often junk food, too) ("Paul claims Hot Doug's serves chazerai, but I think the beer is talking.")*

4. **Ferblunget:** *(get) lost ("Paul got ferblunget on the way to lunch.")*

5. **Fermisht:** *confused ("Paul is fermisht about where we're going.")*

6. **Fershnooshkit:** *drunk, Paul's usual state. ("That guy is fershnooshkit.")*

7. **Hok mir nisht ken chainik:** *don't make me crazy (literally: "don't hit the tea kettle") ("Oy, hok mir nisht ken chainik, Paul, and please stop talking about the Miami of Ohio lady's volleyball team.")*

8. **Kine horah:** *the magical phrase uttered to ward off the evil eye; also, the phrase uttered to show that one's praises are not contaminated by envy. ("Kine horah, Paul can sure drink a lot of beer.")*

9. **Shandeh:** *a shame ("It's a shandeh Jill married a Hoosier.")*

10. **Shnorrer:** *someone who you invite for the weekend and stays two weeks ("I told Paul to come to Hot Doug's for a bratwurst. Fifteen foie gras sausages later, the shnorrer finally went home.")*

place where you could get all of them. I really liked the idea of a restaurant with a single focus—this is what we sell, and this is all we sell, and we're not trying to be everything to everyone. It was a shot in the dark, but I threw caution to the wind. (I say that, but also I was in the fortunate position of not having kids and living below my means. My grandfather taught me at an early age that if you make $100 a week and you spend $101, you're in trouble.)

Quitting the Gig

I remember going into my boss's office and asking if I could close the door. Her immediate question was, "Are you quitting?" I gave her six weeks' notice. And I started looking for a location.

I really started thinking about what I wanted: a Chicago hot dog stand with local, neighborhood people running it—nothing computerized, no nameless person taking orders. I wanted the garish colors, the kitsch on the walls. And I wanted to listen to my records all day. It didn't need to be in the heart of a bustling neighborhood; in fact it was better for it to be just a little bit out of the way. Just a place where you could eat lunch for $5, where you could get good sausages, hot dogs, and fries, and that's it. I wanted to make it the kind of place that I would want to go to. I didn't need it to be for everyone in the city, just a tiny percentage of people.

My family and friends were pretty supportive. There was a certain amount of dubious thinking involved, but by the same token, it wasn't that crazy. I'd worked in restaurants before and gone to culinary school. My mom was a little skeptical, and my brother was like, "Don't you think you need to sell hamburgers?" (My response: "I'll know in six months.")

My dad just said, "OK." In fact, it was my dad who came up with the name Hot Doug's. We were sitting at breakfast and I was telling him about it (I figured I should let him know some of the plans, as he was helping with the financing). The working name was Schleppy's: The Bulvan. Bulvan means hearty, boisterous person, which came from the Hot Dog Club and a sentence that Paul had used in the report. As I was telling my dad about this, he replied, "Yeah, yeah, but what about Hot Doug's?" Hands down the best decision I have made is not calling it Schleppy's: The Bulvan. I bought the URL for Hot Doug's and started incorporating under that name.

I quit my job in April 2000 and opened in January 2001. When I quit, I had no space, nothing. Within eight months, the restaurant was open for business.

A Question for Corny's

In those eight months I had off, I looked for a space. I wouldn't say I looked really hard—I did enjoy sleeping in, and there was a lot of daytime television I hadn't seen in a number of years. For some reason, I started looking in Evanston first, seduced by the Northwestern University demographic. With the help of a real estate agent friend, I found a dry cleaner in a small strip mall whose lease was expiring. I went to the Evanston town hall and started researching the process of developing the space for a restaurant. Once I started looking into the renovation costs, I quickly realized it would be way more expensive than I had budgeted. So instead, I set about finding a place that was already a restaurant. I walked around, drove around, and looked at a bunch of empty restaurant space.

I lived in Roscoe Village at the time. At the west end of Roscoe Street was a restaurant called Corny's Dog House. Every time I would go past Corny's, it was closed. People comment that the current Hot Doug's has lousy hours and is often closed for vacation, but this place was truly never open. No one was ever there. It was literally a two-block walk from my house. At that point it was summer of 2000. This area of Roscoe Village was practically abandoned; there were

STRAUSS SURGICAL GROUP ASSOC, S.C.

4646 North Marine Drive • Chicago, IL 60640 • 773-564-6200 Fax 773-564-6200

To Whom It May Concern:

I have known Douglas Sohn for very many years. In fact, since he was born. I have always had great hope for him. He has always proved to be way above others of his age group and school group. When he discussed that he was going into the hot dog business, I suggested to him a name for it. I suggested "Hot Doug's" and being a very smart individual, he took it on and used that name for his business. I told this to a number of individuals after this and they suggested that I also tell people that I also named him Doug, which was kind of prophetic. Had I named him Henry, it would have been called Hot Henry's, which does not seem to have the same pizzazz to it as Hot Doug's.

To pay me back for all this great work of giving him the name of his restaurant, he told everybody that "even my dad stands in line," which means that I have to wait in line just like anybody else to get into his restaurant. However, I must admit I do not feel bad about this in as much as I listen to people rave about the great food and the great attention that Doug gives them when they get inside. I congratulate him on the great work he did. He did it by himself and these are the kind of entrepreneurs that we need in America to bring back the economy. Thank you.

Sincerely,

Herbert Sohn, M.D.
Date Dictated: 7/18/2012
Date Transcribed: 7/20/2012
HS/17647
Job#: 68494441

DOUG'S RESPONSE:

I DO NOT, REPEAT, DO NOT MAKE MY DAD STAND IN LINE. THIS IS HIS CHOICE. AND I'M PRETTY SURE HE DOES IT SO HE CAN TELL EVERYONE IN LINE THAT HE'S MY DAD. HAVING SAID THAT, I HAVE HAD TO TELL HIM TO STOP BRINGING ME NON-HOT-DOG-RELATED JUNK FOR THE DÉCOR, ALTHOUGH I DO LIKE THE VIAGRA CLOCK (HE'S A UROLOGIST).

old beat-up houses and pretty much nothing west of Leavitt. My brother suggested I just go into Corny's and simply ask them if they wanted to sell. Here was the conversation:

> Me: Are you interested in selling?
> Owner: Who are you?
> Me: I'm interested in buying.
> Owner: Did you see the ad?
> Me: No.
> Owner: Here's the price. I'm leaving for Hawaii at the end of the week. Let's get this done before then.

Nick Markos, Jill Oldham, Hot Doug, Paul Kelly, and Leah Yarrow (full, junior, and guest members of the Hot Dog Club).

PHOTO BY ROYA JADE

The Original Hot Doug's in Roscoe Village.

I was intrigued, but I couldn't answer quite that quickly. I told him to go to Hawaii, let me do what I needed to do, and then we'd probably have a deal when he got back. I bought it for what seemed like a serious amount of money to me, but later I realized it was almost a pittance. I got half the equipment—the other half belonged to the landlord—and renegotiated the lease. I signed on for five years, and the owner of Corny's gave me a tour of where he bought his inventory. It was really nice and he was very generous.

I bought the place in November, and opened in January. I tried to open for Elvis's birthday on January 8, 2001, but it didn't work out. There was too much cleaning, painting, and general fixing-up that needed to be done. That seems like a million years ago. It was a whole different ballgame.

CHAPTER 2

Starting Up: The Original Hot Doug's in Roscoe Village

The Logo

O nce I started telling my friends about my decision to open a sausage restaurant, I would guess that many of them were somewhat doubtful (and possibly concerned that my experiences in the 1980s had finally manifested themselves into a not-so-pragmatic state of mind). Many of them asked, "What can I do to help?" I'm not the type of person to ask for help, so my normal reaction this question is, "Thanks, but I can do this myself." Fortunately, I had the good sense to ignore that instinct, and instead took people up on this offer. ¶ My friend from high school, Judine O'Shea (who is still only 27 years old—no matter what year it is when you're reading this book), is a graphic artist and textbook designer. I told her the restuarant needed a logo.

THE LOGO DESIGN

Doug asked me to help with the logo and gave me a greeting card to use for ideas. "Absolutely!" I responded, and put the card in a super safe place. It turned out that this place was so super and safe that when I went to draw the logo it was clear the card was lost. I looked in everything: stacks of paper, inboxes, file cabinets...nothing. So we proceeded anyway, and the day we presented the completed drawing (by Carrie Gowran) to Doug, he loved it! We were good to go.

That night I opened a book and there was the card, right in the first few pages. The title of the book? *Last Train to Memphis: The Rise of Elvis Presley*. Of course that's where I put it; anyone who knows Doug knows he loves the King.

And of course, for the opening of his restaurant, I gave Doug the Elvis record of "Hot Dog."

—JUDINE O'SHEA

Here's an alternate version from a different friend.

BY B. A. ROSENBLUM

She knows me well and has known me for a long time, which is why the logo sports heavy-rimmed glasses and red gym shoes, a look I chose around 1978 that fortunately hasn't gone out of style. (It hasn't, right?) Also, I'm not naked (there's mustard) and I'm holding a bag of fries. These are two things I'm mostly doing (or not). She gave it to me, and I said, "That looks cool!" And I went with it.

I remember reading a newspaper article about a hotel that spent well over a million dollars to redo their logo, and it's basically the name of their hotel but with a line through it. This same article also talked about a successful local hot dog shop's logo and the owner said something like, "I spent $200. I gave the artist $100 before and $100 after." Of the two methods, I figured I'd go with the latter. If you are reading this Judine, it's possible I still owe you $200.

"No Two Finer Words..."

My friends Nora and Robbie Butler were living in the Chicago suburb of Lake Zurich, which I think is actually closer to Switzerland than Chicago. A group of us would go out there every so often, just to snack and hang out. One day, in the summer, we were at their house—I think it was the time we were deep-frying a turkey, but generally we just deep-fried everything we could—and we started talking about sausages.

Robbie, in his infinite wisdom, said, "There are no two finer words in the English language than 'encased meats,' my friend." This was in the early '90s, when I was in culinary school, and

This was the original "No Two Finer Words..." painted by Chris Posdal at the first location.

I always remembered it. I wrote a paper for my History of Gastronomy class called "Encased Meats, My Friends: The Sausage in History." And when I was opening the restaurant, I called Robbie and asked him if I could have the slogan. He said I could and I trademarked it; I didn't give him any credit in the trademark application, either. This will probably come back to haunt me, but I'll worry about that later.

ONE OF MY FAVORITE STORIES ABOUT THE QUOTE: A CUSTOMER WAS AT YANKEE STADIUM WEARING THE HOT DOUG'S T-SHIRT WITH THE QUOTE ON THE BACK. HE HEARD A WOMAN LAUGHING BEHIND HIM, TURNED AROUND, AND REALIZED THAT KIRSTEN DUNST WAS READING THE QUOTE AND LAUGHING. I HOPE HE TOLD HER SHE WAS REALLY GOOD IN *THE BOURNE IDENTITY*.

NOTE: ROBBIE IS NICKNAMED "SECRET ROBBIE" BECAUSE I KNEW NORA FIRST, AND FOR A LONG TIME, I'D HEAR ABOUT THIS GUY ROBBIE. I HAD NEVER MET HIM, AND I DIDN'T KNOW IF THEY WERE DATING OR WHAT. IT WAS ALL VERY SECRETIVE. AND THEN ONE DAY THEY WERE ENGAGED. I'M STILL A LITTLE SUSPICIOUS.

HOT DOUG'S

The Sausage Superstore

2314 W. Roscoe

1 block east of Western Ave. in the heart of Roscoe Village

773.348.0326
call for hours

fax your order: 773.348.0488

There are no two finer words in the English language than "encased meats," my friend.

The Original Menu

When the restaurant opened in 2001, we didn't have the same menu we have now. We had our regular menu, the Game of the Week, and the Jackie Bange & Mash, which was sausage and fries.

THE FIRE DOG WAS A CHALLENGING ONE TO NAME (AND CONTINUES TO BE). THE NAME HAS CHANGED OVER THE YEARS, LIKE MANY OF THE DOGS, BUT FOR THIS ONE, THE PROBLEM IS TWO-FOLD: (1) YOUR FEMALE ENTERTAINERS OF THIS ILK HAVE A TENDENCY TO GO OFF THE RAILS VERY QUICKLY, AND (2) I HAVE A GENUINE FEAR OF APPEARING TOO CREEPY. I'M NOT A YOUNG MAN, YE' KNOW.

THE DOG: This, my friends, is why it all started. It was the focus when I opened, and it's still the focus now. And it's still my favorite thing on the menu. When it's done well, it's awesome. The flavors, the textures, the whole mouth feel, and the fact that it's $2. Delicious.

THE ELVIS: He's the King and I'm a big fan.

THE LARRY POTASH: Naming the brat after Larry was a blatant (and, it turns out, successful) attempt to coerce the local news station to come into the restaurant. Larry was, and is, the WGN-TV morning news anchor.

THE BRITNEY SPEARS: I do like handsome young ladies, and I wanted to appeal to the youngsters out there.

THE ANN-MARGRET: I also like the handsome not-so-young ladies.

THE VITO MARZULLO: I'm a Chicagoan born and raised, and I love the local political scene. I think of Vito Marzullo as the quintessential Chicago alderman of my youth.

PJ SOLES: PJ is my all-time favorite actress. Riff Randell, rock 'n' roller.

THE ROBIN MEADE: This was combination of trying to lure the local media and a fondness for handsome women. This one worked too. I still swoon a bit from the two-handed handshake Robin gave me when I appeared on NBC's Weekend Morning News. I met Anna Davlantes, too. It was a good day.

PHOTO BY JOHNNY VILLALOBOS

THE GAME OF THE WEEK: I knew that there were lots of unusual sausages available with different animals involved and I needed to fill up the menu.

THE RICK REUSCHEL: I love baseball. By birthright, I'm saddled with rooting for the Cubs. Rick is my all-time favorite baseball player for two reasons: (1) he was the best player on the teams of my youth; and more importantly, (2) I love the fact that a guy with relatively the same physique as myself could be a dominant athlete.

THE HOWARD DEVOTO: Howard is the cofounder of the Buzzcocks, one of my top five favorite bands. He may or may not be a vegetarian.

THE CHARLIE SOHN: Charlie is my nephew. I hope one day he or his brother James (born since the first menu) will come work with me. I probably won't have to pay them the going rate.

My nephews James and Charlie Sohn enjoying the closest thing to a good hot dog in the Bay Area.

THE JACKIE BANGE & MASH: Apparently I had absolutely no shame when it came to sucking up to the local news media. It was my friend Mark Schwarz who came up with this pun on the British bangers and mash (sausage and potatoes). And yes, this one worked as well.

FRESH-CUT (NEVER FROZEN) FRENCH FRIES: This is still true. We cut fresh potatoes with a hand-cranked cutter every morning.

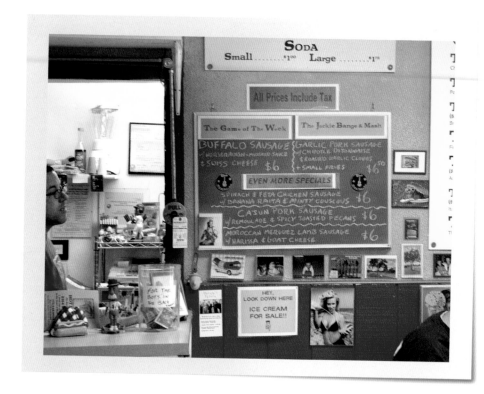

The Jackie Bange & Mash (left) was written on a chalk board at the first location. It eventually came to be what is now known as the "Celebrity Sausage."

This is the second set of menu boards at the original location. Other than some of the names, the only change was replacing the chorizo with the Thuringer (bottom left). Other than that, it's pretty much the same menu that exists today.

This is about as crowded as it would get in the early days. Also, I'm not behind the counter, because I'm probably out front bringing the food out. Yup, used to do that, too.

DOUG'S TOP 7 FAVORITE GAME SAUSAGES

(In no particular order)

1. **KANGAROO**
2. **WILD BOAR**
3. **ALLIGATOR**
4. **RATTLESNAKE**
5. **BISON**
6. **SMOKED YAK**
7. **THE MOUNTAIN MAN** (a damn-tasty combination of elk, venison, antelope, and buffalo)

FRANKLY SPEAKING

BY PHIL LOPRESTI

Taste buds burst into delirium
At Hot Doug's sausage emporium.
Alligator, snake and boar
And something ducky for Joe Moore,
And more duck in duck fat fries.
Game of the Week wins the prize.
It's always worth the wait in line
To get cuisine for which I pine.
Doug's up front to merrily vend
the finest encased meats, my friend.

Game of the Week

When I was putting the menu together for Hot Doug's, I did a fair amount of Internet and cookbook research on different types of sausage. Let's face it; I had to have more than three items on the menu. Well, I didn't have to, but if I was proclaiming the restaurant to be the "sausage superstore," I figured it would be a good idea if I did. Fortunately, I came across several sources for different types of game meat sausage. Thus, the Game of the Week was born. I'm always game for a good play on words. (See what I did there?)

KNEW HIM WHEN

Anyone growing up in the Chicagoland area has stories about knowing celebrities before they were famous, about the band that later became Styx playing at their prom, or about playing Little League with Bill Murray. Before Doug's restaurant had arguably the longest lines in Chicago, and before Doug became a world-famous outspoken critic of city culinary politics, Doug catered my backyard party in 2003. I was throwing it during the summer solstice to celebrate the completion of a home remodeling project. I approached Doug on a slow day (yes, there used to be slow days) in the old restaurant about providing the food for the party. Doug agreed and made up platters of sliced sausages with dipping sauces and condiments. That, along with many kegs of beer, made it a very memorable party. Thanks Doug, for great food and great counter discussions over the years. Talk about rising from the ashes (literally)! I'm glad you decided to continue the dream of affordable encased meats for the everyday man! —**DOUG KOLASINSKI**

This is a vampire hot dog I made for the first location. It was on the front door for a month or so around Halloween.

—CHRIS BACH

Search "hot dog" on eBay and pages and pages of hot dog crap will show up.

I mentioned pages and pages of hot dog crap, right?

Please don't ask me which ones these are. I'm not saying they all look alike, but...

I still tear up thinking about the Madonna posters on the ceiling that were destroyed in the fire (Chapter 3). Years of collecting down the drain (sort of a mixed metaphor, but they didn't actually go up in flames).

There have obviously been no advances in applying condiments to hot dogs.

Back when we were young. I vaguely remember those days.

The days when we only had one fryer. Please don't tell the health department about the leak.

Fortunately, virtually all of the current hot dog paraphernalia is now donated to Hot Doug's. Not that there is a theme of "less work for me" or nuthin'.

Cash Only

That's right, we're cash only. There are basically two reasons why: For one, it's a whole lot simpler to just take cash. (With Watergate, the answer was "follow the money." With Hot Doug's, it's "follow what makes Doug's job easier.") A lot of what we do has a throwback theme: one store, one item, simple process. While I'm neither a "mom" nor a "pop" (to the best of my knowledge—there are a few weekends in the latter part of the 20th century that I simply can't account for), I like to stick with that simple, easy feeling.

The second reason is that I think people should carry cash. I'm kind of stubborn about this. Also, even at a low rate, why should I give a portion of our money to the CEO of some damn bank that is too big to fail? It's a little bit of a mistrust of large corporations and banks. While we've run into people not having cash with them, and I do enjoy the look of utter shock that comes over them as they realize it's cash only when they've gotten to the front of the line, it's still not really an issue. No one has ever left hungry when they don't have cash. We also accept sweat equity and anything edible or potable (I am particularly fond of single-malt Scotch).

But let's face it, my mother told me, and I know your mother told you, that you should never leave the house without 20 bucks in your pocket. Yes, I know it's the 21st century and everything is being paid for with credit cards, debit cards, and PayPal accounts, but I'm telling you that as long as Dick Cheney is alive,

HOT DOUG'S: THE EARLY DAYS

BY ANDREW SOHN
(FORMERLY JUST HERB SOHN'S SON, BUT NOW KNOWN AS HOT DOUG'S BROTHER)

While my memory is considerably less than perfect these days, this is what I remember. Doug had been formulating this idea for a place that would serve only hot dogs and other sausages for a while. And all I, or anyone else for that matter, knew was that the restaurant would serve only sausages—no hamburgers, chicken breast sandwiches, salads, just sausages. And Doug had only doubters. "What about the group of coworkers who go out to lunch and one guy wants a salad?" people would ask. They would pose it as a question, but it was really just their way of telling Doug that his idea would never work and that he would never, ever succeed. I suppose that during those first few weeks the only people who would come in for lunch were some kids from Lane Tech, people from the Walgreens on Western, a few folks from WGN, and that was about it. That never-ending line really did seem to form over night.

My brother is really an amalgam of all of those business clichés and maxims about hard work, focus, believing in your dream, marching to the beat of your own drum (or that drummer in the Buzzcocks), all that sort of stuff. I can say that I knew him when he was a temp for some association management company, when he worked at a cookbook publishing company (A 1,001 Gooey Desserts), when he was doing God only knows what, and when he hid in the phone-booth at his elementary school while all his classmates took the tour. But no one is more proud of him now than me.

PHOTO BY WENDY GUNDERSON

DOG-WALKING ROUTE

I started going to Hot Doug's back in 2004, when I had a dog-walking route in Roscoe Village. I was vegetarian and hated most condiments, so what business a girl like me had at an establishment like Hot Doug's, well your guess is as good as mine. Regardless, I regularly walked out the door with two plain grilled veggie dogs with cheese, and a smile on my face. I told all of my friends about the wonders of Hot Doug's and dragged them there at every opportunity. Now I live in Minneapolis. I only make it back to Chicago about once a year, but every time I stop at Hot Doug's to get my fill. I have six-month-old twins and I'm counting down to when they're old enough for their first trip to Chicago for some Hot Doug's. It's a tradition I can't wait to start! — **JULIE CANDY**

WHOEVER THIS GUY IS

I grew up on great hot dogs from the original Yo Joe's on Addison and Narragansett. After they closed, I really missed my hot dogs. Hot Doug's original sausage superstore was just a few blocks from my house in Roscoe Village. Although I had lived in the neighborhood for several years, I had never eaten at Hot Doug's because it always closed at 4:00 p.m. Finally, I had a Monday off for a holiday, so I went and had lunch served to me by the new hot dog maestro, Douglas Sohn. I was instantly hooked. Besides the great food, what I enjoyed the most was the happy and pleasant manner, and the quick and wicked sense of humor. When my parents came in town, I chauffeured them right from O'Hare to Hot Doug's. I proudly introduced my parents to Doug and he said, "You have a lovely son. I'm not sure who this guy is, but I'm sure you have a lovely son." — **MARK FERRANTE**

THERE IN THE BEGINNING

Hot Doug's has a different meaning for me. You see, I am one of Doug's first-ever customers. (I tell a lot of friends that I was actually the first customer—that may or may not be true.) I believe it was January 2001. I was a junior at Lane Tech High School, which had open campus lunch for upperclassmen. My group of friends and I would always go to different places for lunch. One of the guys in the group mentioned that there was a new hot dog place on Roscoe that we'd have to check out.

I remember walking in and no one was there, a far cry from the hour-long line that exists today. Doug greeted us, and we exchanged some kind of pleasantries about the Britney Spears poster he was hanging up. After getting a run-down of the menu, I chose something simple: a deep-fried dog with fries. It was heaven on earth. Doug sat with us and chewed the fat. We loved the place; my friends and I went nearly every day until we graduated. I never really strayed into the exotic sausage side of the menu, but everything I have ever eaten at Doug's was great (God bless the Thuringer).

The best thing about Hot Doug's is Doug himself. He really cares about what he does. Even though I only make it back once a year, and haven't been in over two years now, Doug remembers me. He'll give me a handshake when I get up to the counter and he'll say, like he did in when I was in high school, "What are you havin', E?" I'm sure Doug doesn't remember my full name, but it doesn't matter. I try to offer him legal services in exchange for food and line-cutting privileges, but Doug has yet to succumb.

I feel a sense of pride for Hot Doug's. I was there at the genesis, and I am super glad that it has become as successful as it has. The only thing I regret is not going there more often. I think I'm afraid Doug won't remember me, but I know that wouldn't be the case—maybe I'm just afraid of waiting in that line!!! — **ERYK FOLMER**

DO NOT LEAVE A PAPER TRAIL. I like not being beholden to the banks. I like the idea of there still being businesses that do it this way. If you go to New Orleans, for example, there are tons of places that do it this way. I also like the idea of paying for something and not getting the bill three weeks later.

We don't have Wi-Fi, we don't have flat-screen TVs (or screens of any other thickness), and we don't take credit cards.

Apparently enough people carry cash, as we're not out of business. I've only have had two jackasses give me grief about this in 12 years, one of whom did not understand that a debit card was not the same thing as cash. It might be cash to a customer, but it's not to my business. For the amount of money I would have to pay in transaction fees, it's not worth it. It's not money that's going to charity or filling the potholes on the street in front of my house. It's going to CEOs and presidents of banks who have screwed up a lot in the past several years. It's creating, not curing, the national debt!

And have I mentioned it's a whole lot easier on my end?

PHOTO (LEFT) BY JOHNNY VILLALOBOS, (RIGHT) BY KARDAS PHOTOGRAPHY

The Duck Fat Fries

Just after graduating culinary school, and about five years before Hot Doug's opened, I did a culinary tour of France and Italy with a group of both recent graduates, like myself, and current culinary students. I left for France about a week before the tour was scheduled to start and met my friends Greg Baker and Gail Connelly in southwestern France. They took me to a restaurant in Bordeaux called La Tupina, which featured a bubbling cauldron of duck fat over a wood-burning fireplace in the center of the restaurant. They would cook a lot of things in this cauldron. For example, the restaurant's amuse-bouche was tripe deep-fried in duck fat (as in, animal fat fried in animal fat). They also did frites—small potatoes cut to order on the wood table in front of the fireplace, which were then fried and sprinkled with fresh thyme, cracked black pepper, and sea salt. Needless to say, these were the best french fries I've ever had in my life.

A short while after I opened, I did some research and found I could get buckets of rendered duck fat from the Hudson Valley in New York. So I had some shipped to the restaurant, then bought a tabletop home-use deep fryer at Target and put it in the restaurant. And we started cooking up duck fat fries, just on Fridays and Saturdays. We cut the potatoes on a plastic mandolin. Quite honestly, I wanted to do it for fun and for myself. They started to gain popularity to the point that I had to start keeping a list of names and bringing them out one by one. It would sometimes take a half hour to get to the bottom of the list. We eventually upgraded to a commercial tabletop fryer, which worked for a while. Finally, at the new store, we ended up buying a regulation-sized fryer dedicated solely to duck fat. We still cut them thinner than our regular fries. We still only sell them on Fridays and Saturdays. I often get asked why. Well, because (1) it's just one more thing we gotta do and each additional task is pretty much a pain in the ass, (2) we are naturally more busy on the weekends anyway (I suppose this is a chicken-and-egg situation), (3) the exclusivity of offering them only on the weekend generates a bit more business (you have to come back—see what we did there?), and (4) duck fat is expensive. We want to maintain low prices and keep a small staff. All right, I'll be honest; it's mostly just because it's one more thing we don't have to do Monday through Thursday.

DUCK FAT FRIES

For your culinary enjoyment, Hot Doug's is proud to serve
"Les Frites en Gras de Canard de G.Baker"
(Fresh-cut potatoes fried in rendered duck fat)
Served Friday and Saturday only $3.50

This original sign is by Mark Bello.

Hours, 10:30 a.m. – 4:00 p.m.

I knew I wanted to do something 9–5. There was never a thought of expanding those hours. I knew how restaurants could take over your life very easily and quickly. So my goal was to either do it in this time frame or go do something else.

We were originally going to open at 11:00 a.m., but one day before we opened, we were in the restaurant and one of the Lane Tech High School kids stopped by. He said that the first lunch break was at 10:40, so we opened at 10:30. I always knew I would close at 4:00 p.m.

I remember in year two, I tried staying open until 7:00 p.m. on Thursdays and Fridays—that lasted about three weeks. I think on two of those six nights we ended up closing early due to lack of business.

But it's mostly so that I could keep it as close to a 9–5 job as possible.

We started out opening five days a week so I could have a little time to get my feet wet before opening Saturdays, which we did after about three months. Other than those three weeks of late closes, and those first few months of no Saturdays, it's been 10:30 a.m. until 4:00 p.m., Monday to Saturday. One time we closed early, at 2:00 p.m., so I could go to my house closing. We've never opened late, and we are hard-core about closing at 4:00. I like to think that between 10:30 and 4:00 we're the nicest restaurant in Chicago; at 4:01, heart of stone.

TOP 3 ANSWERS TO "WHY DO YOU CLOSE AT 4?"

1. **Unfortunately, it's not financially viable to close at 2.**

2. **I don't go to your job and say, "Hey, you should work longer!"**

3. **We were supposed to stay open 'til 8, but the sign maker put 4 and I didn't feel like getting a new sign.**

The Press

When we opened in January 2001, there weren't things like Yelp, TripAdvisor, or billions of food blogs. I didn't have a PR agency because of ignorance and budget. I just didn't know enough about the restaurant business at the time. I did, however, know that I wanted to have time to work out the kinks, to make sure it was running the way I wanted it to run, and to not be overwhelmed by customers.

Looking back, keeping things simple was the right thing to do. We were able to open in a quiet way. We took over an existing spot where no one went, so the first few press clippings were minor publications. They were very complimentary; not raving, but they were good. They noted that we did some unusual things, and that it was a limited menu. At that time there were only two notable restaurant review sites: Metromix and CitySearch. On one of those we had something like 10 reviews in the first couple of months. Nine of them were pretty positive, and one was bad—and it was that one that made me nuts. From that point on, and to this day, I have never read another review. I figured that if people stopped showing up, then maybe I'd go online and see what was going on.

OK, that's not totally true. A friend of mine will often forward one-star reviews to me. My two favorites have been the one that complained that the venison sausage was "too gamey." The other gave us a poor review because he came after 4:00 p.m. and we wouldn't let him in. I love the Internet!

> Hot Doug's is on the edge of Roscoe Village, on a not-quite-rehabbed block, nestled between a Seventh Day Adventist Church and a hair salon.
>
> The walls, painted by Sohn and friends, are ketchup red and bright mustard yellow with touches of Play-Doh blue. The tables are tilted, Elvis is venerated in framed photos. The hot dog in the logo has glasses, very much like Sohn's own skinny black retro rectangle frames. In the window there are hot dog in bun lights, and there is hot dog paraphernalia (acquired from friends and through eBay) at the counter.
>
> Sohn is the front person, taking orders, dressing the sausages and putting on the condiments, while his one employee does the frying and grilling. Behind the counter hangs his associate's degree in culinary arts from Kendall College, from where he was graduated about six years ago.

CITYTALK, APRIL 6 2001,
(BY SL WISENBERG)

> Calling Hot Doug's a hot dog joint is like describing Mr. Jordan as another shooting guard.
>
> Hot Doug's décor is tastefully selected, with artwork leaning towards Elvis memorabilia. An array of ex-Cub Rick Reuschel baseball cards sits over one table; a Viagra wall clock hangs nearby.... Elvis Costello or Lou Reed blast out on the stereo, the better to munch a dog to.

LOCAL PALATE, NOV/DEC 2001,
(BY ERIC FUTRAN)

> That's right, Hot Doug's serves up fresh-cut potatoes fried in duck fat. It may sound harsh, but they taste so damned good you'll forget all about how they got that way...Doug's regular fries come thick, fresh cut and crispy in all the right places, making them a neighborhood favorite as well.

RED STREAK, MARCH 18 2004,
(BY MICHELLE BURTON)

THERE ARE PRESS CLIPPINGS THAT ARE GREAT FOR BUSINESS AND THEN THERE ARE ARTICLES THAT MAY OR MAY NOT HAVE AN EFFECT ON BUSINESS, BUT MOST DEFINITELY HAVE AN EFFECT ON THE EGO. THE PUNK PLANET ARTICLE IS THE LATTER. IT WAS CERTAINLY ONE OF THE FIRST ARTICLES ABOUT HOT DOUG'S TO APPEAR AND IT IS STILL ONE OF MY FAVORITES. TO BE CONSIDERED PUNK STIRS UP THE 17-YEAR-OLD-KID, RAMONES-LOVING ETHOS I STILL STRIVE TO MAINTAIN.

punk planet
notes from underground
issue #50 July & August 2002 $4.95 US

The Mekons | Tortoise | Innocent on Death Row | Venus Zine | Martin Sorrondeguy | Homocore

welcome to
CHICAGO
richard m daley, mayor

Being a vegetarian hasn't stopped me from falling in love with Hot Doug's, a year-and-a-half old hot dog stand in Chicago's Roscoe Village.

Boasting a sausage-only menu that could make a grown man weep (this week's special: wild boar sausage), Doug Sohn's decidedly down-home storefront stays packed during its

would do *this* the way these guys do it, or "I wouldn't do it like those guys because they are totally lacking." That kind of thing led to me thinking, "Well, *I* could do this." That's really how it started. ¶ I never had *any* intention of owning a restaurant. I wanted to stay in the food business, but I had no desire to open a restaurant. As a matter of fact, that same person who had the bad hot dog—I blame him for a lot of things—about two or three months after I first opened, we were

chatting and he said "Remember when I was thinking about opening a Bar-be-que restaurant? Do you remember what you said?" I said, "not really." And he says, "You said never, ever, ever, ever, *ever* open your own restaurant." [*laughs*] I was like "Where the hell were you three months ago?!" ¶ Additionally, I wanted to do something different and get out of the office. I finally decided to take a shot at it and see how it goes.

In this city there are a lot of high-end gimmick restaurants—the place where everything's on toast, or everything's on mashed potatoes, or everything is made out of oranges. You coming from a culinary school background, it seems like the obvious choice would have been to follow those leads and open a high-end gourmet hot dog restaurant. But instead, while you're serving some stuff that isn't normally served at a hot dog stand, you have the form, pricing, and everything else of a hot dog stand.

True. That was certainly part of the original plan. I didn't want to exclude *anybody*. The term "gourmet" always gives me the shivers. You know what? It's a hot dog. It can be a good hot dog, but *anyone* should be able to afford it. I also wanted a place that you could come in and have lunch for five bucks. There aren't many places you can do that. You can't even do that at McDonalds, really. Here, you can get two dogs, a small fries and all the Coke you can drink for five dollars even. That was really important to me. Yeah, I have the game sausage and other fancier things, but I wanted to make it accessible for anybody. There is certainly a place for high-end restaurants, no doubt about it, but I didn't want to limit myself to a particular clientele. Hot dogs are the every man's food. A good hot dog is still better than a bad duck breast with cherry sauce and wild mushroom risotto.

So what made you decide to make it above and beyond a normal hot dog stand? You've got wild boar sausage on the menu right now. Last week you had rattlesnake . . .

We've done alligator, we've done ostridge, we've had kangaroo, and we've had chicken sausages of different varia-

tio...
sau...
ex...
fo...
m...

what owning your own
that's been tough. There are a phenomenal amount of headaches; a phenomenal amount of stuff that breaks. Learning how much everything costs—every little, *tiny* thing costs money. The first six months were a phenomenal amount of stress. Having never owned my own business, I had no idea. Being in publishing before this I had dealt with deadlines, but that's *nothing*. The lack of sleep and loss of weight the first six months were unbelievable. Now it's much better, but there's still always something. It's taught me *much* more than I thought it would.

Can you see doing this for the rest of your life?

I have no idea. Five years ago, I never thought I'd be in this position. Honestly, I try not to look too far ahead at this point. I just have to see what happens next. But certainly if it works, I have no problems with that.

There are a lot shadier ways to earn a living than slinging hot dogs.

Absolutely. I have no moral qualms at all making a good, well-priced lunch for people. I have no problem with that at all. ◉

The term "gourmet" gives me the s... You know It's a ho...

Doug Sohn takes a break from sling...

PUNK PLANET'S 50TH ISSUE

"Are you sure you haven't gone crazy?"

That was my girlfriend doing a sanity-check as I told her I wanted to interview a guy that ran a hot dog stand for the magazine I ran, *Punk Planet*. It was our 50th issue, which we were theming around the world of independent music, culture, and politics in Chicago. I'd actually just come back from doing the last interview for the issue that was going to press in just days and had stopped off at this hot dog joint I'd seen on my route back to grab a bite.

That joint was, of course, Hot Doug's—in its original location on Roscoe—and from the moment I sank my teeth into a veggie dog done up Chicago-style I knew immediately that our issue wouldn't be complete until the guy behind the counter, Doug Sohn, was in its pages as well. I walked up at the end of the meal, introduced myself, and asked if I could come back the next day to do the interview.

Maybe it was a little crazy, but the hot dog means a lot to this town and so does doing honest work well. To me, sitting there eating that dog, listening to Doug give gentle shit to each person that came through the door, seeing him and his guys in the back busting ass to make the best lunch in the world, nothing could have been more Chicago.

It's been more than a decade since that day. That Hot Doug's burned down and a new one opened up. The girlfriend that called me crazy is now my wife; we have a kid who's been a celebrity sausage. And yet after all that time, I walk into Doug's and it feels exactly the same: there's Doug, every day, giving gentle shit to everyone, there are his guys—many of them the same ones as all those years before—busting ass in the back, and there, in front of me, is the best lunch in the world. —**DAN SINKER**

Mr. Sohn's place of business is more than it seems at first. In his irreverent moments, of which he has many, Mr. Sohn describes it as an encased-meats emporium. Rightly so. It serves a fine Chicago red hot...but also what you might describe as canine nouvelle cuisine. At Doug's you can order a veggie dog or a kangaroo sausage if you like....

Doug's, of course, was hors classe. A converted storefront in Roscoe Village, a middle-class residential area on the North Side, it was jam-packed at 3 o'clock on a Saturday afternoon, with a line out the door.

NEW YORK TIMES, APRIL 14, 2004
(BY R.W. APPLE, JR)

In any case, I'm very thankful that I could follow my simple plan and still be successful. We wouldn't be able to do that today; the Internet and social media have really shaped the restaurant business in the last 12 years, particularly in Chicago. There is a tremendous online focus on restaurants, and everyone is very opinionated, which just wasn't the case when I started. A little bit, but not like today. Restaurants today get reviewed before they even open. Now it seems almost impossible for restaurants to survive long enough to get into their groove. Some people are living their dream and working really hard, but they get one bad online review and they're done.

I may not understand how someone can find a venison dog too gamey, but I do understand that if you're going to charge a customer full price, you have to give them full service. You should be ready to go the moment you open your doors. I hope that all my customers, whether or not they were satisfied with their meal, can walk away feeling that they were served well and charged fairly.

I still don't have a PR team, though.

THE CARTOONIST

Way back in the early days of Hot Doug's, when it was empty enough that I could sit around after my meal and draw my cartoons, I would watch Doug banish customers (mostly high school kids) for incorrigible language or behavior. It impressed me to see a guy who was willing to kick people out of his new, struggling business.

That sort of pruning permitted him to grow a clientele that cares about the entire dining experience. The simple courtesies of maintaining an orderly line, closing doors to keep the heat or the AC in, and refraining from occupying tables until an order is placed contribute to an egalitarian atmosphere and a spirit of community. Obviously, it is also great business. If only more businesses had such discipline. It took Doug years, after all, to build a following loyal enough to create—and then endure—the legendary long lines.

I remember standing in line in the rain with my older daughter when she was only two. I said we were a couple of crazies. The next time we came, she asked me if we were crazies. I said, "No, it's not raining this time." So she asked if the other people in line were crazies. The man in front of us turned around and confessed, "I am. I drove all the way from South Dakota." Just for a hot dog.

Except not just for a hot dog. For an entire experience. And a community. Even if it is (arguably) a community of crazies.

At least they're nice crazies. And that's what keeps us coming back. — **PAT BYRNES**

Pat Byrnes is a cartoonist for The New Yorker *and author of the book (and blog)* Captain Dad: The Manly Art of Stay-at-Home Parenting.

HOT DOUG'S, INC.

Hot Doug's really marks a whole generation of Lane Tech alums. I remember being introduced to the original location my freshman year by some older kids I used to hang around with. Everything they did was cool, so Hot Doug's was definitely cool. When I finally found a group of friends in my year, we bonded over Hot Doug's. We would push through the mêlée of hundreds of students pouring out of school for lunch, power walk to Hot Doug's, scarf down some hot dogs, and give ourselves stitches in our sides as we raced back to class. We went practically every day and called ourselves Hot Doug's Incorporated, a name we took from a letter framed on the wall next to our table.

Even though I wasn't friends with the older kids anymore, the fact that Doug always knew my name (and still does to this day) and my order (though I converted to vegetarianism somewhere in there) made me feel like one of the cool kids. There are so many stories I can tell about this place: how it's become the default reunion spot for meeting old friends; how I once cheated on vegetarianism for a hot dog, and no one who hasn't been to Hot Doug's understands why; and how my friends (most of whom have moved from Chicago) and I agree that Hot Doug's is quintessentially home. Also, I have a really hard time saying "Doug" instead of "Hot Doug" when I talk about him. — **JACQUELINE LYON**

Hot Dougs Rules!!!

HOT DOUG'S RULES!!!

This picture is courtesy of Dorrie Craven, age 10. She (and I) have been coming to Hot Doug's for almost all her life. The original location on Roscoe was a good walk from our house, and just far enough to justify eating the french fries once we got there. My favorite memory of Hot Doug's was when Dorrie was just starting to eat "real" food, and liked sliced tomatoes. I asked for a small side dish of tomatoes, and Doug presented her with a small fry container full of tomatoes for her very own, and refused to take money for them.

—GWYN AUBREY (AND DORRIE AND JOHNNY CRAVEN)

Guest Cashiers

When we started opening Saturdays we got busier and busier. There were just two of us at first. My friend Gary "The Glove" Manning was my first, and, for a few months, only employee. He helped prep, cooked the fries, lifted the heavy things, cleaned, and generally did all the things I didn't want to do. He's now a Chicago cop. Coincidence? Draw your own conclusion. I'd take the order, ring people up, help cook, and then take the food out. I started asking friends to be guest cashiers. They'd take the orders, I'd cook, and then I'd take the food out. My brother Andy; Nick Markos, the composer of "Theme from Hot Doug's"; Jennifer "The Rooster" Oosterbaan (easily the best-looking one); and Peter "Vic" Kousathanas all guest cashiered for me.

Guest cashier Jennifer Oosterbaan. (PHOTO BY NICK MARKOS)

GUEST CASHIER: JENN

I'm not going to lie. It's very likely that I agreed to be one of Doug's guest cashiers in a bar, after several beverages. That said, when he called me in the cold light of day and reminded me of my promise, I didn't hesitate. After all, it's impossible not to get wrapped up in Doug's passion for encased meats, and he was my first friend to open up his own place. It seemed incumbent upon his friends to pitch in and try to help make it a success. Also, he promised me a free t-shirt. Anyway, how hard could it be?

Of course, what I didn't know when I reported for work that bright and sunny Saturday morning was that the night before, Doug had received the first of many rave reviews on a local television station. In fact, I found that out from my customers, who formed a line out the door from the minute I got there to the minute we closed. Many of them had traveled from far-off places, like the suburbs. Who knew a good sausage could make people do such things? Clearly, Doug did.

My stint as guest cashier is a great memory. Not only do I feel like I was there for the beginning of the love affair between Hot Doug's and Chicago's most ardent sausage fans, but it was the first of many weekends when I would meet up with the other kids in Doug's crew to while away the hours over duck fat fries. If there's a better way to spend a Saturday afternoon, I can't think of it.

— JENNIFER OOSTERBAAN

GUEST CASHIER: PETER

Nick Markos, a good friend of mine from college, introduced me to Dougie back in '92. I really didn't know what to think of the guy when I met him. He was personable, quirky, and comically gifted with a lightning-fast deadpan delivery. But he was odd—funny, but odd; a bit of a maniacal madman, know what I mean? I thought, I better keep an eye on this guy.

Dougie had this stooge-like, hairbrained scheme to open up a hot

single self-respecting Greek father who owned a diner sat his kids down and said if they ever opened a restaurant, Dad would personally strangle them. So I'm thinking to myself, here's two smart college-educated guys with "real" jobs sitting in a ghetto flop at Pierce and Paulina, talking about opening up a hot dog joint. Absurdist nonsense! What are they thinking? Romantic nonetheless.

Fast-forward a few years. The

ber feeling really proud of him as soon as we walked in. We sat down, engaged in a decent shit-talk session, had some laughs, waited for what seemed like a slight eternity, and finally we were served some amazingly delicious dogs. It was a very pleasant and cordial experience; however, I must admit, I had the uncanny feeling of being in the basement of a church, or in a shrine, some dubiously holy place. It was quite odd. As we were leaving, Dougie mentioned that he could use an extra hand on Saturdays. It was his "busy" day. He requested that I come in and guest cashier. I had just retired from the envelope business and was already bored out of my mind, so I jumped at the opportunity.

A few days later I show up to "work" early for my obligatory tutelage session. Doug's already there, getting things ready. We exchange some morning pleasantries, he cracks a few jokes, and then he

Guest cashiers Nick Markos and Peter Kousathanas.

dog stand that only served encased meats. This struck a chord with me; I used to dream about shit like this too. I guess it was in my blood. However, I had been warned. I grew up in an environment where every

esteemed Mr. Sohn has gone through a variety of gigs, and then one day I hear he's opened up the wiener stand. So a few of us friends get together and we go down to Roscoe Village and check it out. I remem-

starts the lesson plan. Now keep in mind the joint is tiny; we're talking 30 square feet of work area or something like that. We're completely on top of each other. He says he needs me to take the order from the customer, run the register, serve the goods, clean up some tables, etc., etc. He mentions that there will be plenty of downtime, so keep myself busy and stay clear of him, 'cause his jokes are gonna get old fast. I feel I'm pretty prepared; after all, this isn't my first rodeo.

Just before we open the doors, Doug realizes he's neglected to mention one thing. He grabs a small stack of 3x5 index cards that are cut in half and hands them to me. I say, "What's this?" He says that this is what he wants me to write the order down on. I say, "Whatya mean? Ain't you got no green restaurant check pads or somethin'?" He says that the index cards are cheaper, plus we can recycle them and use both sides. Wow. He's either a real pragmatic utilitarian or he's got serious commitment issues. Perhaps he doesn't think he's gonna be around long enough to use up a whole check pad. Then again maybe he's just one cheap son of a bitch... probably a combination. So I say, how do you want me to do this? He says, you know, write down what they want, hot dog w/_____, Polish w/_____, K for ketchup, M for mustard, etc. I look at him and I'm thinking, he's within earshot of the customer as they order. He's right behind me, for fuck's sake. We're in 10 goddamn square feet of space. I'm barely a formality in this equation and he wants me to give him

CH DOL - M, RO, R
SCDOL - (EV)

THUN - BM, CO, P

BUFF - BM, CO

LF

a 2½x3-inch index card with the Magna Carta inked on it? Wow, this is guy is fucking wound up tight!

Half an hour after the doors open, a punter finally comes up to the register, orders a dog with everything but relish, fries, and a root beer. Easy enough. I figure, Dougie hears the order and he'll start making it. Not so. This pale-faced, non-Hellene infidel chef is simply glaring at me. I think, maybe I should repeat the order for good OCD measure. That's not gonna work either. He's still staring me down. I give in and write everything down, call the order out, hand him the stiff little card, show him the bullet points, and rehash the details. He loosens up a bit and makes some wisecrack about "How Jesus saves and Moses invests." Finally, he arches his eyebrows up four inches, pops his eyeballs over his Absurdistani-styled

eyewear, and stares at me for a long, hard, silent minute...like he doesn't trust me with the details of the order that he himself overheard just seconds ago, or like I'm gonna screw him over at the register or something...like he's thinking "I've got my eye on your slippery little fingers you greasy Greek." After a few more long stares at me, then at the index card, then at me again, he musters up the nervous energy, confidence, trust, courage, or who knows what, and starts working on the order.

Wow, this is gonna be one fucking long day. This guy is delusional if he thinks he's gonna be here running this joint much longer. I mean first off, there are three of us in the joint "working." Gary the Glove, a reformed graphic designer, is on deep fryer detail, sinking spuds into the hot grease. I'm at the register and on table cleanup. Master Doug is on hot dog duty. Three fucking guys taking care of what may be five customers per hour...the money-making math is looking dismal already. I'm a volunteer and I'm already feeling the pressure of the accountants breathing down Dougie's neck, telling him, "Mr. Sohn, it's time to shut the doors and go back to the cookbook biz."

What kinda fuckinguy (sic), with barely any restaurant experience,

opens up a hot dog joint serving nothing but encased meats in a town where 5,000 other dog, beef, sausage, and pizza puff parlors already exist? Ten things on the menu, maybe, max, in a neighborhood where most of his customers are bewildered Lane Tech High School students looking to inject a greasy gyros into their esophagus. They come in asking for pizza puffs, no pizza puffs, burgers, no burgers, beef, no beef...just dogs and sausages. Like I said, I spent years working in Greek diners growing up, all my friends worked in them, their dads owned them, ran them, we all started when we were six years old. We know what it takes to make a joint work. You need a 13-page laminated menu with 2,500 items on it that can all be served piping hot in six minutes or less. That's how you fucking make money in the restaurant biz. Or so I thought.

A little while later, the door opens and in stumbles this middle-aged, heavily haggard local dipsomaniac. It's just before noon and this dame's lit off her fucking rocker. She starts weaving up to the register as if slaloming through some imaginary line of customers on her way up to order her grub. She slurs out her order and I oblige the boss's request with my penned version of an acrimonious diatribe on the miniature card. We go through a slightly adjusted variation of the aforementioned

shenanigans and finally he starts preparing the woman's repast.

There's nothing else for me to do so I turn sideways, keeping one eye on the lush and one on Dougie. He seems to have shed his nervousness and stepped into a bit of a groove. It becomes quickly evident that the master has gone into a trance-like state. He reviews the index card, procures and gently splits open the Mary Ann bun, gingerly inserts the steaming Vienna dog, then looks back to the index card. He's fixated on the card. Finally, he looks up, throws his arms out like a maestro, his shirtsleeves creeping up his forearms, and the wizard starts dressing the dog. He grabs a hold of the mustard bottle with both hands, props his hips up against the edge of the counter, stands up on his toes, and starts squeezing out the yellow condiment. At this point he's no longer dressing the dog, he's *decorating* it. Oh my god, this fuckinguy's opened up the world's first sausage decorating superstore! It's the Saturday noon lunch rush and we've got an audience. There are four and a half mesmerized customers on the other side of the counter who aren't sure if they've just witnessed Chicago's first officially unauthorized wiener molestation ritual, or a madman chef practicing for his pastry finals at Le Cordon Bleu. The cantankerous, beer-soaked broad is getting anxious. She approaches the counter

and plops down some loose change with one hand, and with the other hand she reaches over and snatches the frank from the startled prima donna. Off she went! Dougie turns to me, his saucer-like eyes wide with disbelief. "What happened?" he incredulously gasps. What happened?! I'll tell you what fucking happened! You just spent half the morning overzealously decorating a goddamn culinary masterpiece. Meanwhile, you've got a slew of hungry customers waiting to down some dogs and be on their merry way. This is how you're gonna run this joint? What a debacle! When I left there that day I thought maybe he'd keep the place open for another week.

Those were the early days. There weren't anywhere near enough people to form a line, but Dougie, the unintentional chaos theory poster child, had created an inadvertent queue. By using subversive guerilla marketing tactics, like meticulously squeezing out mustard as if he was piping butter cream frosting onto marjolaine, he took half an hour to fill a goddamn hot dog order. He kept the customers artificially waiting. What initially could have been perceived as an uncomfortable and awkward situation attributed to the growing pains of working in a new field, actually became a precursor to perfection. Well played, Ace.

In a twist of comical irony, years later I get a phone call from Dougie. "Uncle Vic, I need some order tickets for the cooks."

I say, "Whatya mean you need order tickets? What happened to the index cards?"

"We're way beyond index cards, my friend!" He replied.

"Well, how many you need?"

He threw out a number that almost made me gag. I told him he was nuts. I called up an old printing buddy of mine and we got the job done. I couldn't believe how many order tickets I was delivering. A few months later he calls me up again and wants to reorder. I ask him if people are stealing them, if there was flood damage, a fire loss, what the hell's going on. He chuckled on the other end of the line and said he had simply run out.

Thank heaven Dougie got out of the kitchen and moved to the helm and started shit-talking with the customers. God only knows what woulda happened if he had stayed back there decorating wieners.

My mom was a great cook. Whenever I used to compliment her on one of her superb meals, she would, without hesitation, state: "It's the ingredients, not me!" Well Ma, as it turns out, it's not just the ingredients. It doesn't hurt to have a bit of quick wit, funny glasses, and a love for Joe Strummer to pull off a culinary coup.

Here's the takeaway from all this. Be passionate about what you're doing. Believe in yourself and your vision. Surround yourself with a good team of characters that get it. Give customers the best that you can give them. Open the doors and people will come. Keep doing it right and they'll keep coming. This is Chi-town, and solid efforts get rewarded. Hot dogs have been around for ages, sausages even longer. They weren't invented in Chicago, but I'll be damned if Dougie didn't perfect them! And when the time comes, in true cult-like fashion, shut the fucking doors to the sausage shrine, and hang up the "closed for good" sign. Let the Japanese tourists, the out-of-town businessmen with their waiting cabs, and the remainder of the faithful lament the loss for an eternity. Turn yourself into a modern day Gauguin. Beach yourself on some remote atoll in the South Pacific and enjoy the spoils of success before we all kick it one day!

— PETER "VIC" KOUSATHANAS

NAME: CHINT

Qty	Item	EV RO	M CO	K R	BM T	DM P	HONEY HP	CHEESE GIAR	PLAIN KRAUT	CS	CHILI	
	ST DOG											
2	ST DOG	(EV)										
	CH DOG											
1	CH DOG	(EV) RO CO				(HP)						
1	POLISH	(M) R CO T							CS	(CHILI)	CHTRD
1	FIRE	(EV) RO CO					(GIAR)				
1	BRAT	(CO)		(BM)				(KRAUT)			
	ITAL										
	THUR										
1	ANDOU	(CO) T (P)		(BM)							
2	VEG	(EV) RO									
	CHIX										

1	VEAL	—	(No BUN)
2	FOIE		
1	ATOMIC	CU, ITABAN	(CHIP-SIIC)
2	SHRIMP		
1	LAMB		

___CORN   ___VEG CORN   ___BAGEL/TOTS

(1) SM FRY   (1) SM CHEESE/CHILI   ___SIDE CHEESE
(2) LG FRY   ___LG CHEESE   ___DUCK FRY
___SM TOTS   (1) LG TOTS

HOLD   **(GO)**   SODA 3ᵗ

59

FOUGHT DOG BY DAN GRZECA

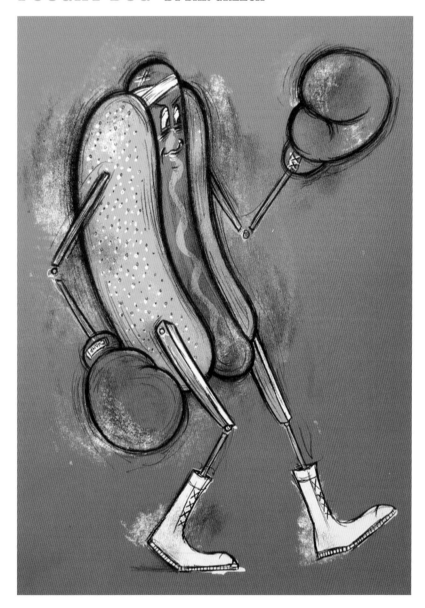

LIFE LESSONS

Try as I do to be a good role model for my two young sons, Owen and Faris, one Saturday I really let them down.

That Saturday started off as many do, with a plea from the boys to go to Hot Doug's for lunch. They know the importance of leaving the house at 9:30 a.m. to be first in line. Initially I resisted their pleas because I was several months into a rigorous fitness schedule with dietary restrictions. Hot dogs and carbs were out, salads with low-fat deli meat were in. I decided to pack a quick salad, not sure if bringing food into Hot Doug's was allowed.

Before placing my order I asked Doug if such madness was allowed. Ever the gentleman, Doug said it was fine (though I secretly hoped he would say no). I proceeded to order some dogs and fries for the kids and we sat down to eat.

I unpacked my lunch, overly sensitive that my lunch sack looked like a man purse. As I began eating my salad, I could tell that something was bothering Number 1 Son.

"What's wrong, champ?" I asked.

I could tell he was struggling with what he wanted to tell me. He said, "I just want you to know that I don't think it's cool that you're eating a salad at Hot Doug's. I mean, it's HOT DOUG's. It's not a place for salads and I hope you don't ever do this again."

I looked over to Number 2 Son and asked whether he had a similar view, but he was too busy eating his chili cheese fries.

"You're right," I said. "This won't happen again."

Now we have a metaphor: "Bringing a salad to Hot Doug's" serves a reminder of the types of bad choices we should avoid in life.

— JIMM DISPENSA

HOWARD DEVOTO DEVOTEE

My first Hot Doug's experience was at a *Punk Planet* holiday party in the early aughts. It was my first stop of the night, not as a slight to Dan Sinker, but because he promised food. So I was there on time—too early for any party—and sat in a corner, sipping a beer as a few other guests walked around the office. Doug Sohn came bursting in, hauling a mess of tin and buns and condiments. He plopped them on a table and said, "These are meat. These are veggie," and left to talk to Sinker. I had friends who were big fans of Doug's but I had never gone. Like many punk rockers of the 1990s, I was a vegetarian and didn't think Hot Doug's was for me. Well, this holiday dog was a delicious veggie dog, so I was determined to see the real thing.

Soon after, I went. At the time, the veggie dog was called the Howard Devoto, a nod to the first singer of The Buzzcocks. That was awesome. Fear was playing over the PA. That was also awesome. I went again. And again, ad nauseum. We passed by one day to see that Hot Doug's was closed and a man was cleaning up some debris outside. We asked what happened. The man said, "There was a fire." So is Hot Doug's closed? I mean, it looked perfectly fine, despite some tiles falling from the ceiling. "Yes, and I don't think he's opening again." We were devastated.

When Hot Doug's reopened, I started taking my friend Matt, who was a huge Devoto/Magazine fan. We ate there a lot, even skipping work specifically to come to Hot Doug's. Once, a stranger took a photo of me buying the Celebrity Sausage and put it on LTH Forum, leading me to get busted by my coworkers. They were understanding. Our friends Norah and Jay and Keara and Benetti and Poindexter and Dan Sinker were somehow always there. In 2005, I walked into Hot Doug's and took in the rest of the menu that wasn't the Howard Devoto (then renamed the Steve Diggle). The different toppings on various sausages and duck fat fries just took over my appetite. I had flirted with fish earlier in the week, so now it was time to dive headlong into Hot Doug's menu. I had a rabbit sausage, a garlic pork sausage, an Italian sausage, and a regular ol' Chicago hot dog. Ten years of vegetarianism ended right there.

There are three things I suggest to every out of towner: (1) take an architecture tour from the Chicago Architecture Foundation, (2) get a drink at the top of the John Hancock, and (3) go to Hot Doug's. —VINCENT CHUNG

CHAPTER 3

Closing Down: The Fire

The Hazards, The Fire

The physical plant of the first Hot Doug's was not exactly what one would call "up to code." A dump is probably more precise. When I took over the restaurant from Corny's, I found a few issues. For example, the drain for the soda fountain well was literally a garden hose running though a hole in the floor, with the runoff spilling into the crawl space in the basement. This was right next to the runoff that went directly from the hand sink to the crawl space. To drain the three-compartment sink in the back, someone had drilled a hole directly into the sewage pipe. You're not supposed to do this. We also had a problem with the electricity; several of the lights and equipment would flicker on and off. So we called an electrician, who pulled the meters out in the basement, at which time we were able to determine that the wires behind the meters were singed and slightly smoking. We also noticed that a lot of the wiring was done with extension cords running across the basement ceiling.

The whole building was a mess. The restaurant was on first floor of a three-story building that had a small apartment upstairs and a large three-story apartment in the back. The family that lived in the back when I opened was a couple and their two ne'er-do-well 20-something sons. (One of whom once asked me for advice about his girlfriend who was f*cking around on him, which was OK, since he was f*cking around on her, but she was also f*cking around with this same guy's dad, at which point I told him, honestly, "I have no idea what to tell you. Truly. I have no idea.") The older woman who lived in upstairs was on oxygen, and her staircase was filled with oxygen tanks. I often saw her sitting on the bench in front of the restaurant smoking cigarettes with her oxygen tank right next to her.

The family in the big apartment eventually moved out, and the landlord began to rehab the place. He decided to do the work himself with his friends. Over the course of the next four months or so, we would smell paint fumes and hear hammers pounding—you know, the usual renovation noises. They seemed to be progressing, and nothing was out of the ordinary.

The evening of Saturday, May 1, 2004, we were hosting a wedding shower (back when we did that kind of thing) for a friend from a previous job, Kerri. Throughout the day, we had been smelling paint fumes and turpentine, but that wasn't unusual or cause for concern.

The party was going smoothly and beginning to wind down; we had served the food, cleaned the kitchen, and turned off the gas. Right about the time when the couple was opening their presents, I smelled something. My friend Lisa, who was helping out as a server that evening, turned to me and asked if I smelled smoke. I looked up and said, "Yes, I do, because it's coming out of the light fix-

> " I walked out the back door and looked up to see huge flames pouring out the second-floor window. Glass was shattering, black smoke was spilling out; I'd never seen anything like it."

WIENER SHOWER TURNED FIERY DISASTER

If there is one thing that my friends and I know for sure, it's that a wedding is best entered into with a handful of hot wieners. With this guiding principle, my friend Joanna Spathis planned our couples wedding shower at our favorite wiener stand, Hot Doug's.

It was the perfect choice; Hot Doug's had been a big part of my early relationship with my now-husband, Martin Barron. Doug opened right around the time Martin and I started dating, and we were frequent visitors. We were even some of the lucky few to enjoy Doug's dinner hours back in his early days.

Our shower started out wonderfully, with Doug and his workers churning out sausages to our hearts' (and stomachs')

delight. Little did we know that the hot-doggity joy we were feeling was about to turn into a crushing fear as we asked the question, "Will Hot Doug's ever return?"

Anyway, wieners were eaten, presents were unwrapped, friends were hugged. Someone said, "Do you smell smoke?" "Nope," I replied. Then—with perfect sitcom timing—smoke started coming from the ceiling.

I remember turning to Doug at some point and saying, "You have all of these people here. Should we grab some of your stuff?" He answered no, that we should just to get out safely. (This question would haunt in me in the months ahead, when we would drive by the smoky ruins of the old place and see the

beloved memorabilia still lining the walls. Why didn't I just grab the stuff anyway?)

Most of our cars were blocked in by the numerous fire engines, so we had no choice but to watch with horror as it became clear that this was no little blaze that would be over in a few minutes. Knowing Doug's love for his business and our love for his business, I'm not exaggerating when I say this was a terrible realization.

Once Doug's was back and better than ever, though, it did become quite a nice little piece of cocktail party banter, telling about the night of our wedding shower, when we watched Hot Doug's 1.0 burn.

—KERRI KENNEDY

SHOCK TO THE SYSTEM

The fire was a horrible shock to my sausage-loving system! We drove by the old spot and saw the boarded-up windows.

We patiently waited for some cleanup and reconstruction, but there was none. Then His Sausageness informs the public that he's looking for a new spot.

So I was one of the people who would email Doug every time I found a location that would be perfect for him. And Doug was kind enough to reply back to tell me what was wrong with the

location I suggested. Undaunted, I just kept sending emails, begging him to reopen.

It was a long wait, but our prayers were answered when Doug announced he would be reopening on California and Roscoe. The new place is much larger, and I guess I've gotten over not having a TV there so I can watch the Cubs play (during day games).

And during the Hot Doug-less time, we discovered that no one has anything that comes close to the fine quality of sausage Doug serves, nor with the wit and humor of His Sausageness himself.

—LEE BERENBAUM

The bride and groom blissfully drinking Cokes before the fire started.

Fire trucks douse the building while guests watch across the smoky street.

tures." I remember Kerri's father shouting "Oh my God," and getting everyone out. They grabbed the presents, and everyone shuffled right out front. Then fire engines started coming. I walked out the back door and looked up to see huge flames pouring out the second-floor window. Glass was shattering, black smoke was spilling out; I'd never seen anything like it.

I ran around to the front of the building and told one of the firemen about the staircase filled with oxygen tanks—in my mind the building had now become a missile silo.

For the next two hours, I stood under the awning of the building across the street (it had started to rain) and just watched. About four blocks of Roscoe Street had been shut off to traffic. The fire department command unit had set up right near the restaurant. I was quite impressed that the people who board up windows had gotten there almost as quickly as the fire department. I called the landlord to let him know what was happening. He said that at 4:00 p.m. everything was fine. I told him that at 7:30, not so much.

Finally after a couple of hours I went up to one of the firemen. I told him I owned the restaurant on the first floor and asked him if I was out of business. "Oh yeah," he said, "you're done."

Next Day...and Months

I don't really know exactly what happened, but I'm pretty sure it had to do with the welding and sparks and embers and turpentine and two-by-fours—you know, the things that could make a building a tinderbox. Luckily, the restaurant only suffered water damage; the equipment was stainless steel, so it was OK. The freezers and coolers were OK. The Madonna posters on the ceiling (a collection spanning almost 15 years), though, did not survive. (These were the same Madonna posters that a young mom once took me to task for, saying there were inappropriate images in the restaurant. It took me a while to realize she was talking about these posters. I kept saying, "But, it's Madonna.")

So the day after the fire I was out of a job. The good news was that everyone was OK. I happened to be moving the very next day; after 14 years in my apartment in Roscoe Village, I was moving about six blocks away. I barely remember it because I was so stunned—I was definitely in shock for a little bit after the fire. I remember going to the building the next day and hav-

BURNT OFFERINGS

I was introduced to the wunderkind known as Doug Sohn through my fellow gluttons at Tower Records. (Remember Tower? Remember records?) The memory about Hot Doug's that immediately stands out in my mind doesn't involve any of the great meals I've had there—complete with duck fries and Green River soda!—but one that I missed out on. Back when Doug was at his old location in Roscoe Village, my friend John Lazar and I dropped by for lunch on one of our regular visits. As we approached the establishment, we noticed something was amiss; the lights were out and the door was ajar. As we got closer, we detected the smell of smoke—not the welcoming aroma of encased meat sizzling on the grill, but the stale funk of an extinguished inferno.

Still not putting two and two together, we entered and found Doug talking to an insurance investigator, surrounded by the aftermath of a fire that had gutted his business. As we gazed at the burned-out interior, we turned to Doug and asked the most moronic question imaginable under the circumstances: "Are you open?"

Hungry and clueless...always a winning combination.

Since that calamity, Doug has bounced back and Hot Doug's is better than ever. Yet it took a while for him to regroup at his current Avondale location. I eagerly anticipated a grand reopening, but as time dragged on, I felt like a convicted governor (pick one), checking days off a calendar while awaiting parole. And I cursed Doug for not serving us lunch that fateful afternoon. I mean, why didn't he? Those sausages were roasted anyway. —**TED OKUDA**

ing the overwhelming sensation that it looked kind of like those old World War II photos of bombed-out buildings. Giant holes in the floors and ceilings, charred beams, and puddles of water.

Fire shutters hot dog joint

MONDAY, MAY 3, 2004
EDITION: REDEYE PAGE 7
DATELINE: ROSCOE VILLAGE

The autographed picture of Britney Spears is undamaged, the Viagra clock continues ticking and the fryer where owner Doug Sohn cooks his french fries in duck fat survived unscathed.

But Hot Doug's, a popular hot dog restaurant in Roscoe Village, will be closed indefinitely after a fire last weekend in an apartment upstairs severely damaged the building.

Sohn, who opened the restaurant three years ago and has since cultivated a large and loyal customer base, said he is looking for another storefront in the same area.

Neighbors can hardly wait.

"The whole neighborhood is freaking out," said Dave Schmitt, 37, who lives about a block from the restaurant at 2314 W. Roscoe St. "It's a cultural thing to do in Roscoe Village."

Sohn bills the restaurant as serving "the finest in encased meats." He has drawn local and national attention for his extensive sausage menu—rom simple corn dogs and bratwurst to more elaborate offerings, such as last week's special: cognac-infused smoked pheasant sausage with sauce moutarde and truffle cheese.

A Fire Department spokesman said the blaze was started by a welder refurbishing one of the building's apartments.

For the next few months I fixed up my new home, watched *The West Wing* reruns, went out to lunch, accounted for all of the stuff at the restaurant, did a boatload of paperwork, and fought to get my payment from the insurance company.

And of course I had that big question hanging over my head: Now what do I do?

Reality set in that I'd lost my restaurant, that everything I'd worked to create was gone, just like that. My initial thought was, "Sweet, I'm out." No more of this restaurant nonsense.

But as the insurance payment was just not that great, I still had to do something to make a living. And I could never really come up with anything else I wanted to do. At one point during that summer, I considered partnering with other people and franchising the restaurant so that there'd be several locations. We got pretty far into it, even going so far as to incorporate, but after awhile I realized that I really didn't want to do that. I just didn't want to have more than one restaurant. That's not who I am. That's not what Hot Doug's is. And if I was going to have only one restaurant, I guess I felt that I didn't need partners. I like to think we parted on good terms (we're still friends), but this is something that I could and wanted to do on my own. And yes, I'll admit it, I really don't like having other people make decisions I'd have to abide by.

The Reaction

I spent a good part of that summer doing nothing. Every so often, I would get a call from or run into a customer asking me how was I doing, and whether I had any plans. My favorite memory is once when I was driving down Southport with the windows down, I heard a disembodied voice shout, "When are you going to reopen?" I'm not saying this was an "if you build it, he will come" moment, as I'm pretty sure the shout came from a person on the sidewalk and not a voice from the great beyond, but it was pretty humbling. I also turned down a Hot Doug's fundraiser event, as I have a moral opposition to fundraising for a for-profit company. Nevertheless, I was incredibly flattered. The outpouring from friends and customers that summer totally swayed me into trying this nonsense one more time.

CHECK'S IN THE MAIL

I had spent a huge sum of money to outfit the original Hot Doug's with three, maybe four team pennants from games we had gone to (upwards of maybe $20), including pennants for the Chicago Rush, the Chicago Wolves (I believe there was a Calder Cup pennant for them), and the Schaumburg Flyers. They were lost in the fire. I am still waiting for the insurance settlement.

—PAUL KELLY

Merle Gordon

Dear Doug,
As a huge fan of Doug's Dogs, I was devastated to read about the fire. So this is just a short note to let you know This fan is thinking about you and sends wishes for a speedy resolution to your relocation. (I'll be checking The website for updates.)
The very best to you—
merle Gordon

WITH DEEPEST *sympathy* AND PEACEFUL *wishes.* for a quick reopen!
OH NO!
JUST DROVE 5 miles to get a big treat — what a shock! Come to my neighborhood— great spaces on Grand/May & Morgan/Aberdeen area
BEST WISHES FOR reopen MARY FLEMING

HOT DOUG'S, AS SEEN FROM THE OTHER SIDE OF THE COUNTER BY NISSA HOLTKAMP

I

When I reached the halfway mark, the stranger
Leaned in and said, "It's BYOB, but
You have to bring one for Doug." We lingered
In line, not making eye contact again.

On a crisp March day, armed with Alpha King,
Spring just beginning, I pulled a bottle
From the plastic black bag. Doug graciously
Said, "You don't have to share, Nissa." But I

Did. (How he still remembers and rightly
Pronounces my name, I don't know.) A teen
Lethargically wiped poppy seeds from trays
And tables. Unsettled uncrowdedness,

I mulled over Madonna, her bejeweled
Bikini and enjoyed my sauerkraut
Thuringer and fries. Then, with a striped scarf
And winter flapped hat, local lore walked through

The door. They ordered char dogs (I think) and
Doug asked for the name. Did he really not
Know? Was this courtesy? I nervously
Fixated on the red oval basket.

II

More of a kiss than a crash. The police
Would say it was a minor collision,
If that, if they'd been there. The car crept back
And wap. I hit the white beater behind

Me parallel parking on the south side
Of Roscoe Street. Lucky me, the guy was
In the car. It was his mom's car and it
Had just been fixed. And she'd be so sad to

See the counterfeit dent in her bumper.
Dizzy-headed, I gave him 30 bucks
From my pocket, looking at the first work
Of a trailer hitch, flustered and unfed.

III

We slowly drove past the certain awful
Rumor. Dark soot stains on the siding in
Cirrus smoke curls from the window frames. The
Family above, the hair salon to the

Left. The dirty sunshine yellow awning
And fresh pine boards. The stinging bitter smell
Of dank molecularly changing manmade
Materials. The staff, their families.

Seasickness in an abruptly emptied
Space. Volta. What did it mean? But soon the
Button gumball machine came to line the
Strap of the bag I bought in Italy.

And when water was thrown on my own fire,
Soil ready for regrowth, I came in at
Forty-one weeks. Little hungry William
Could easily outrun me, Doug said, "Are

You sure you want another?" Teasing
Gently. Now, with the smell of leaves muddled
Into the ground, my brewery worker
Works on the other side of Elston. With

Piqued jealous surrender, I told him, "Please
Remember, it's cash only, you have to be
wise and time out lines, thuringers are best,
And if you bring beer, share with the kitchen."

THE REAL CAUSE OF THE FIRE BY MARK BAZER

I stepped into the Hot Doug's line for the first time in the fall of 2002, and was served my first Hot Doug's sausage in the spring of 2003. I will never forget anything about that experience. I ordered the ribeye steak sausage...or maybe it was the spicy Thai chicken sausage...or the elk sausage. I have no idea what I had. I actually remember nothing about that experience, other than that it was exactly like the countless times I've been to Hot Doug's since: sublime, mixed with unappeasable anger and debilitating hunger.

The truth is: Doug changed the way I viewed sausages and, as a result, life. Back in high school, because I know you care about my high school days, we had "open lunch" for juniors and seniors. The thinking was that upperclassmen were mature enough to leave the school for 30 minutes to get high. For those two years, I went every day to a convenience store called Richie's and ordered two boiled hot dogs with *nothing* on them and a large carbonated liquid. This, as much as anything, sadly defined who I was.

The Chicago hot dog (I grew up near Boston) woke me up. But it was Hot Doug's that put the final nail in the coffin containing my timidity. Even if half the sausages Doug serves feature made-up ingredients (duck cracklings?), he inspires you to step out of your comfort zone. Because if you're gonna pay $8 for a sausage,

you might as well as get all the shit it comes with.

Hot Doug's quickly went from a place I'd go to when I was in the neighborhood to a place I'd think of excuses to be in the neighborhood for. Suddenly, the best dry cleaner, Walgreens, and Jewel were all in or near Roscoe Village. Hot Doug's became the place I'd take out-of-town guests who I could stand talking to for an hour or more. It became the place to go when 10:30 a.m. seemed just about right for lunch. And in an age when the two-hour, three-martini lunch is all but dead, the two-hour three-sausage Hot Doug's experience became a more than adequate replacement.

In other words, I ate at Hot Doug's a lot. And that's why in 2004 I burned the place down.

Money, time, an ever-expanding gut. I didn't lack for reasons. I also knew that Doug, always in good cheer behind the counter while the people behind him did work, would find some other calling. Other people, I was sure, would open up comparable, if inferior, "gourmet" sausage places. The hamburger, perhaps, would see something of a renaissance. In others words, Doug would be fine, his customers would be fine, and I could move on with my life.

But Doug, damn Doug, rebuilt. And this time he took precautions—now soaking everything in his restaurant with the same flame-retardant chemi-

cals they put in mattresses. Duck fat, my ass.

Since then, Hot Doug's has only become more powerful in this city. Everyone knows about his foie gras battle, but he has also made sausages out of those Chicago parking meter stickers and TIF money.

I, for one, have taken a new, wiser course in my approach to Hot Doug's. I decided to choose the "become friendly with Doug" approach, instead of the arson one. It took some time, but today Doug and I laugh about what he affectionately refers to as "the time you destroyed my livelihood and sense of purpose." And as great as Doug is at making sausages, he is an even better friend. Which is a shame, because I have other friends and it would clearly be preferable if he were a worse friend but better at sausages.

The lines have only become longer, but I still go to Hot Doug's whenever I need a shirt ironed or a prescription filled. Because for all the sausage competition, gourmet or otherwise, every Chicagoan knows there are only two places worth getting a hot dog: Hot Doug's and the Home Depot at North and Elston.

Mark Bazer hosts The Interview Show *at* The Hideout. *Doug, a frequent guest on the show, is known affectionately by* The Interview Show's *staff as "Don Rickles, if Don Rickles were more offensive."*

The New Location

CHAPTER 4

Hot Doug's Part 2: Electric Sausageloo

New Look

After finally deciding to reopen (and after having seen every *West Wing* episode at least three times—I do loves me some Allison Janney!), I started looking for locations, both by myself and with my brother, Andy. I knew I wanted to stay relatively close to the first location. There simply weren't that many places from which to choose. Roscoe Village was out—too built up, too expensive. I looked into starting from scratch in a space that had never been a restaurant, what the kids refer to as a "vanilla box." I also started researching how much it would cost to build from scratch: hood system, gas line, sufficient electric, and coolers, all that chazerai (I learned that one from the Yiddish Word of the Day). I found a few spots that would possibly work, but quickly concluded that the cost was

MEDIA CONTACTS:
Doug Sohn
Hot Doug's
(773) 279-9550

FOR IMMEDIATE RELEASE
December 2004

HOT DOUG'S REOPENS IN EXPANDED SPACE

Don't Even Think About Ordering a Hamburger

Chicago hot dog fans who like their sausage with a side of shtick have a special reason to celebrate the new year with the long-awaited reopening of Hot Doug's.

More than a hot dog stand, Hot Doug's was famous as a shrine to all sorts of encased meats, with daily sausage specials that ranged from wild boar to spicy lamb. The shop closed several months ago when a fire damaged its original Roscoe Village location. Now it is set to reopen January 4, 2005, at 3324 N. California Avenue, near the corner of California Avenue and Roscoe Street.

"If my customers thought my last location was hard to find, wait 'til they see this one," says owner Doug Sohn. "They should think of it as an adventure into the unexplored wilderness of Chicago."

The new store will have expanded seating and even an outdoor space, which previous patrons will appreciate since lines were often out the door before. Fans of Hot Doug's duck fat french fries will be pleased to know that they remain a menu staple on Fridays and Saturdays.

# # #

way beyond what I wanted to spend. We're selling hot dogs, after all. I simply didn't want to be on the hook for that kind of money. I like sleeping at night.

I found a possible space in the nearby neighborhood of Ravenswood Manor. It wasn't perfect, but I was getting kind of desperate. On the way home, my brother and I took what he claimed to be a shortcut down a street I'd never traveled. We turned south onto California Avenue, into what turned out to be the heart of the Avondale neighborhood. At the stoplight at California and Roscoe, I noticed a restaurant on the corner called Papa George's. It was closed for the day and seemed kind of dark, and, to be honest, kind of dingy (no offense, Papa George). It seemed to be a typical Chicago hot dog stand.

I asked my brother what he thought, and he replied that if I liked it, I should go in and ask the same question I asked at Corny's: "Do you want to sell?" (By the way, I've come to the conclusion that every restaurant in the world is for sale.)

A couple of days later, in November 2004, I went in, bought a soda, and snooped around. It was, in fact, the same type of restaurant as Corny's: burgers, Italian beef, hot dogs—all the classics of the typical Chicago hot dog stand. I was just looking around when one of the customers, whom I recognized as a former Hot Doug's customer, came up to me and asked, "When are you going to reopen?"

"I don't know," I answered, "but I'm looking for a location."

The gentleman behind the counter, who I later found out was, in fact, Papa George, overheard this and asked me, "Reopen what?" After I had given him a brief account of my story, his response was, "What about this place?"

As it turned out, he owned the whole building but was looking to sell the restaurant. Apparently, his brother-in-law had convinced him to open a restaurant for them to comanage, but after realizing it was a boatload of hard work, the brother-in-law bailed a month or two later. Papa George was ready to sell. I guess I was ready to buy.

Within a week we had a deal. He gave me the key, and just like that I owned the space and everything inside. This deal was way better than the first one, where I had owned some of the equipment and the rest had belonged to the landlord. Everything here was mine.

By the way, and I can't stress this enough to anyone interested in becoming a small-business owner: hire a lawyer, hire a good lawyer, and don't sign a thing until your lawyer goes through everything.

One of the first things I did was contact all of my friends who had asked me if there was anything they could do to help. Why yes, yes there was: painting, cleaning, schlepping, furniture arranging, deep fryer calibrating, all the work that's needed to get the business going. We reopened in January 2005.

Congrats'
We are sooo Happy.
Best Thoughts.
see you soon.
John & Cathy

The new place was awesome. We had way more space and we could do more things: more specials, more in-house creations. We could accommodate more people. We had a prep kitchen, we had a basement. Sort of like a real restaurant. Most importantly, things worked: electricity, furnace, hood system, gas line. All of it worked the way it was supposed to work. Some equipment was there, the rest I was able to purchase.

Taking an order (or possibly working on the New York Times *crossword puzzle).*

Giving a food order to the cooks (who may or may not be there, you never know).

PHOTO BY NICK MARKOS

PHOTO BY ROYA JADE

I also had the luxury of knowing how I wanted it to work this time, and I could manipulate the flow of the restaurant instead of just guess and gerrymander as I went along. I could set up an actual assembly line. After three years' experience running my own shop, I was able start over in a better, easier way.

One of the first things I did was redesign the cashier's stand. It was originally part of the cook line; I wanted to separate it so that I wouldn't have to go into the kitchen. If I did, I knew the cooks would want kill me because I would always be in their business. Now, from our respective posts, they can just laugh at me rather than feel homicidal.

My friend and customer from the first Hot Doug's, Mark Bello, is not only a master pizza-maker, but he is also an incredibly talented designer. He created the menu wall for the new Hot Doug's and many other design elements (see pages 79, 82 and 117). My friend Louise Ahrendt offered to paint the murals on the bath-

MENU

The Dog
Chicago-Style Hot Dog with all the trimmings 'nuff said.
$2.00

The Norm Crosby
Chardog: I represent that beef, pork, and garlic.
$3.50

The Elvis
Polish Sausage: Smoked and savory-just the the King.
$3.00

The Joe Strummer
Vegetarian Dog: Meatless . . . and delicious!
$3.00

The Paul Kelly
Bratwurst: Soaked in Beer, sort of like the Paul.
$3.50

The Steve
Chicken Sausage: Classic Italian-style or zesty Sante Fe-style.
$3.50

The Sal Tessio
Italian Sausage: It's not personal, it's strictly sausage.
$3.50

(Pretty darn still got!) The Charlie and James Sohn
Mini bagel dogs and tater tots, the kids love 'em.
$3.00

The Anna Kendrick
Fire Dog: Mighty hot!
$3.00

The Dave Pound
Corn Dog: Deep fried to a golden splendor, it's a sensation!
$1.50

The Brigitte Bardot
Andouille Sausage: Mighty, mighty, mighty hot!
$4.00

ALL PRICES INCLUDE TAX

"Eight months after a fire closed Hot Doug's, the self-proclaimed 'Sausage Superstore' is scheduled to reopen in early January—in a new location. The Roscoe Village hot dog restaurant—a standout even in this city of world-class sausage purveyors—will move about half a mile west, to the Avondale neighborhood. 'I'm looking forward to berating my customers again,' owner Doug Sohn said. 'I've worked up a lot of frustration and anger over the summer.'

CHICAGO TRIBUNE
DECEMBER 19, 2004

room walls (see page 112). I will admit, it's fun to be a patron of the arts; just call me the Lorenzo de Medici of Avondale.

A couple of years after we reopened, I walked by the old location. Some paper had been put up on the windows, but I could still peek in and see that nothing had been done to it. Literally, nothing. The pile of soda bottles we'd moved out of the way were still sitting exactly in the same spot. For close to six years the space sat empty like that. I was curious what the mold count might be. Finally, it was gutted and turned into a nice single-family house. I have no idea if the people inside know it was Hot Doug's or not. No idea. I am kind of tempted to gather a group of 50-odd people on a Saturday morning, and have them form a line out front and demand hot dogs.

An updated duck-fat fries sign by Mark Bello

New menu

I was thinking about changing the names of some of the sausages before the first restaurant closed. So when I reopened, I went ahead and changed the names. And I have done that several more times since. Here is a little chart:

STARTED OFF AS...	CHANGED TO...	TODAY IT IS...
The Dog → (CHICAGO-STYLE HOT DOG)		**The Dog**
The Elvis → (POLISH SAUSAGE)		**The Elvis**
The Larry Potash →	**The Roseanne Tellez** →	**The Paul Kelly**

(BRATWURST) *Originally named the Larry Potash and then the Roseanne Tellez, both WGN-TV news anchors. Eventually I figured I should name something after the jackass who had a bad hot dog and ruined my life (Paul Kelly).*

The Vito Marzullo →	**The Luca Brasi** **The Virgil "The Turk" Sollozzo** **The Frankie "Five Angels" Pentangeli** →	**The Sal Tessio**

(ITALIAN SAUSAGE: It's not personal, it's strictly sausage.) *Originally named the Vito Marzullo, after the Chicago alderman. Decided to go with* Godfather *characters as Eddie Vrdolyak doesn't really sound Italian.*

The Britney Spears →	**The Jennifer Garner** **The Keira Knightly** →	**The Anna Kendrick**

(FIRE DOG: Mighty hot!) *One of the few people to eat her own sausage, Anna tweeted about it in September 2012.*

The Ann-Margret →	**The Raquel Welch** **The Madonna** **The Salma Hayek** →	**The Brigitte Bardot**

(ANDOUILLE SAUSAGE: Mighty, mighty, mighty hot!) *I do likes a handsome woman.*

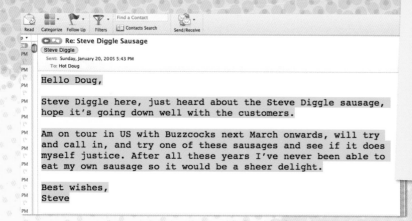

Re: Steve Diggle Sausage
Steve Diggle
Sent: Sunday, January 20, 2005 5:43 PM
To: Hot Doug

Hello Doug,

Steve Diggle here, just heard about the Steve Diggle sausage, hope it's going down well with the customers.

Am on tour in US with Buzzcocks next March onwards, will try and call in, and try one of these sausages and see if it does myself justice. After all these years I've never been able to eat my own sausage so it would be a sheer delight.

Best wishes,
Steve

WHEN I RECEIVED THIS EMAIL FROM STEVE DIGGLE, I (1) DID ONE OF THOSE BOWERY BOYS TRIPLE TAKES AT MY EMAIL MACHINE SCREEN, AND (2) CAME TO THE IMMEDIATE CONCLUSION THAT OPENING THE RESTAURANT HAD TOTALLY PAID OFF.

STARTED OFF AS...	CHANGED TO...	TODAY IT IS...
The Don Rickles →	**The Marty Allen** →	**The Norm Crosby**

(THURINGER) *The thuringer wasn't on the original menu. It replaced the chorizo, which was named the P.J. Soles after my all-time-favorite actress.*

The Howard Devoto →	**The Steve Diggle**	
	The Pete Shelley →	**The Joe Strummer**

(VEGETARIAN DOG: Meatless...and delicious!) *I ran out of Buzzcocks so I had to move on to the Clash. Well, I could've gone with Steve Garvey, but I have a grudge against the other Steve Garvey (Cubs fans will know what I mean).*

The Rick Reuschel →	**The Shawon Dunston**	
	The Dave Kingman →	**The Steve Swisher**

(CHICKEN SAUSAGE) *The easiest sausage to rename. So many Cubs, so much of my wasted youth.*

The Robin Meade →	**The "Psycho" Ronnie Raines**	
	The Ace Patrick	
	The Sally Vega →	**The Dave Pound**

(CORN DOG) *Robin Meade was a local news anchor at that time. Since I got to meet her, I decided to move on and change it to the great roller derby stars of the late '60s and early '70s; another one that's easy to change, and the one pastime that could possibly have wasted my youth more than the Cubs.*

Charlie Sohn →	**The Charlie and James Sohn** →	(Pretty sure still just) **The Charlie and James Sohn**

(MINI BAGEL DOGS AND TATER TOTS) *Originally just the Charlie Sohn, but, thankfully, my brother decided to have another kid, meaning there is even less pressure for me to give my mom grandkids.*

The hot dog clock was a gift from designer extraordinaire Mark Bello.

A fine tray of sausage and the second Britney Spears photo on this page!

If you ask me, this is as long as the line ever gets. I don't know what people are talking about.

Kristina Smith.

I like to point out that both diplomas are honorary.
Didn't even have to leave the counter!

Justin Graham.

Left to right: Eulalio "Lalo" Guijosa, Benjamin Roman,
Octavio Garcia, and Juan "Carlos" Garcia.

Adding the Celebrity Sausage

When we were redoing the menu for the new place, so many customers asked, "Why can't I be a sausage?" and, "Why won't you name a dog after me?" As we have learned, tasks that require additional effort on my end are usually denied. This request would require frequent changing of the menu boards. Not going to happen. Also, most people did not fit into one of these categories:

- **1970s roller derby stars**
- **1970s punk rockers**
- **1970s-to-early-1980s Chicago Cubs**
- **Characters from *The Godfather*, parts one and/or two**
- **Handsome young women**
- **Handsome not-as-young women**
- **Old Jewish comedians**
- **My nephews**

To resolve this, I thought, "OK, we'll have a separate board where we have easy-to-change names and anyone can be a sausage." Often this was for celebrities (and we use the word "celebrity" very loosely at Hot Doug's) who either didn't fit into one of the above categories, or who were maybe not famous enough to achieve a permanent menu item. Or because the celebrity was just a customer. Whatever.

The Celebrity Sausage of the Day quickly became the bane of my existence. It changes daily, so that means I have to come up with five or six a week. I soon hit upon the idea of having a theme for the week and enlisted Paul Kelly (the oft-fershnooshkit Swinging Gentile who had a bad hot dog) to send me a list of names each week. After much cajoling, he actually started sending me lists. He would send six names and I would have to guess the theme. I could usually figure it out, but there were times I was stumped. The problem was that Paul, addled by his

Paul Kelly points at his sausage.

THANKFUL, BUT PICKY

The whole Celebrity Sausage concept bothers Doug, so he'll put just about anyone on there. And yet, he's surprisingly picky and sort of an a-hole about the whole thing at the same time. He wants folks who are pop culture-y and sorta obscure... but only for the things he's interested in. But I'm the one who has to do the lists. —**PAUL KELLY**

PAUL RELUCTANTLY DOES THE LISTS THESE DAYS, AND ONLY WITH A GREAT DEAL OF PRODDING. IT'S MOST OFTEN ME WHO COMES UP WITH THE NAMES. I THINK HE'S JUST MAD ABOUT MY REJECTING HIS LIST OF THE 1972 MIAMI OF OHIO MEN'S CHESS TEAM. I BELIEVE THEY FINISHED 8TH OR SOMETHING IN THE MAC.

beloved beer, would usually forget the theme. So now he includes this with the names. It's not as much fun, but it saves a lot of time.

Paul is from Cincinnati so his lists tend to focus on all things Ohio, whether it's the Cincinnati Reds or graduates of Miami of Ohio University, where he allegedly attended college (like "celebrity," I use the word "attended" very loosely). He's also big on anniversaries (such as the 40th anniversary of the 1972 Chicago White Sox), and obscure band members. He claims that while I say I just want the names and don't care who they are, I then reject 90 percent of them. He may be right about this.

We do try to be topical. Obscure but newsworthy is the goal. We'll do Nobel Prize winners, Bears draft picks, porn stars' birthdays, obscurely famous people who died, I could go on and on. The craziest week was when the New Kids on the Block reformed in 2009. I had no idea what a huge following Joey McIntyre has—the fervor built to the point where people from all over the country were calling and asking for the Joey McIntyre sausage. One woman came in, claimed she didn't eat sausage, but had to have one because it was named the Joey McIntyre.

Paul Kelly's Favorite Celebrity Sausage Lists

GUYS NICKNAMED SPEEDY, SMOKY, AND ROSEY: Speedy Duncan, Speedy Neal, Speedy Thomas, Horace Speed, Mac Speedie, Speedy Claxton; Smokey Stover, Walter Smokey Alston, Smoky Burgess, Charlie Smokey Maxwell, Smokey Joe Williams, Smoky Joe Wood; Rosey Brown, Rosey Colvin, Rosey Davis, Rosey Grier, Rosey Taylor

THE ORIGINAL VH1 VJS (MTV WAS CELEBRATING ITS 30-YEAR ANNIVERSARY): Frankie Crocker, Scott Shannon, Jon Bauman, Bobby Rivers, Tim Byrd, Alison Steele

MEMBERS OF THE 1980s BAND THE JETS (THE BEARS WERE PLAYING THE JETS THAT WEEK): Eugene Wolfgramm, Elizabeth Wolfgramm, Haini Wolfgramm, Moana Wolfgramm, Eddie Wolfgramm, Rudy Wolfgramm, Kathi Wolfgramm, LeRoy Wolfgramm

ACTORS WHO HAVE PLAYED SANTA CLAUS: Edmund Gwenn, Edward Asner, Roy Holmer Wallack, Douglas Seale, Lewis Arquette, Edward Ivory, John Pasquin, Jason Flemyng

GEORGE CLOONEY'S EXES: Karen Duffy, Celine Balitran, Lisa Snowdon, Krista Allen, Sarah Larson, Elisabetta Canalis

ILLINOIS TEACHERS OF THE YEAR: Patricia Adamatis, Laura Stoppek, Linda Smerge, Annice Brave, Kevin Rutter

ELVIS COSTELLO BACKUP MUSICIANS: Mickey Shine, John McFee, Sean Hopper, Johnny Ciambotti, Bruce Thomas, Pete Thomas, Steve Nason

CUBS MANAGERS (AFTER MIKE QUADE WAS FIRED): Rene Lachemann, Bruce Kimm, Joe Altobelli, Jim Essian, Tom Trebelhorn, Jim Lefebvre, Gene Michael, Frank Lucchesi

1970s BEAR WIDE RECEIVERS: Dick Gordon, James Scott, George Farmer, Bo Rather, Charlie Wade, Brian Baschnagel, Bob Grim, Earl Thomas, Rickey Watts

ELIZABETH TAYLOR'S SPOUSES: Michael Wilding, Mike Todd, Eddie Fisher, John Warner, Larry Fortensky, Jason Winters

OFTEN DOUG IS ONLY OPEN A FEW DAYS A WEEK, AND HE NEEDS FEWER THAN SIX CELEBRITY NAMES. ONE WEEK, HE WAS ONLY OPEN THREE DAYS, SO I DID THREE POWER-TRIO BASS PLAYERS: Dale Peters, Noel Redding, Dusty Hill

PEOPLE WHO COULD HAVE DERAILED THE BLAGOJEVICH TRAIN, BUT LOST TO HIM INSTEAD OF BEATING HIM: Mike Flanagan, Roland Burris, Paul Vallas, Myron J. Kulas, Edwin Eisendrath, Nancy Kaszak, Ray Romero

TIGER WOODS'S "FLINGS": Jamie Jungers, Jaimee Grubbs, Loredana Jolie, Mindy Lawton, Kalika Moquin, Cori Rist, Holly Sampson, Joslyn James

CHARACTERS FROM *TOP GUN* FOR THE 25TH ANNIVERSARY*: Sam Wells, Ron Kerner, Bill Cortell, Tom Kazansky, Nick Bradshaw, Pete Mitchell

MARCH MADNESS ONE-SHOT WONDERS: Fennis Dembo, Jai Lewis, Gordon Heyward, Ricky Blanton, Andrew Gaze

SANDRA BULLOCK CHARACTERS (DOUG HATES SANDRA BULLOCK)**: Gracie Hart, Sally Owens, Siddalee Walker, Diane Farrow, Annie Porter, Birdee Pruitt, Gwen Cummings

AMERICAN IDOL SEASON THREE CONTESTANTS WHO FINISHED BETTER THAN JENNIFER HUDSON (THIS WAS BEFORE SHE SANG AT THE SUPER BOWL AND AFTER SHE WON AN ACADEMY AWARD): Camile Velasco, Jon Peter Lewis, John Stevens, George Huff, La Toya London, Jasmine Trias, Diana DeGarmo

1980s NOBEL PRIZE WINNERS: Carlo Rubbia, Simon van der Meer, Robert Bruce Merrifield, Niels Kaj Jerne, Georges J.F. Köhler, César Milstein, Jaroslav Seifert, Desmond Mpilo Tutu

---

* What Paul failed to mention is that we ran this list during Gay Pride week. See, now it's funny.

** I don't hate Sandra Bullock. How could anyone hate Sandra Bullock? She's America's sweetheart. I just think every movie she's ever been in is a piece of junk. Except *Hope Floats*. No, I take that back. That movie stinks too.

WHY I SHOULD BE A CELEBRITY SAUSAGE

For a brief period of time, I was the Celebrity Sausage. I penned the following essay for the Be a Celebrity Sausage contest that Hot Doug's did in collaboration with Half Acre Brewery.
—ERIC HODEK

There are many reasons why I should be the Celebrity Sausage.

First and foremost, I have previous experience as an encased meat. I was a hot dog. Need proof? I've attached some photos of myself for your viewing pleasure to exhibit my unbridled and delicious, juicy enthusiasm. The logical progression for myself from Hot Dog Guy is to Celebrity Sausage.

Furthermore, I am a huge proponent of microbreweries like yours and supporting local businesses (I was actually doing the latter in my role as Hot Dog Guy). And what pairs better with a well-crafted beer than an equally well-crafted sausage? Beer + Sausage = Heaven. I am a fan of your product and microbreweries in general. I have traveled this great land sampling beer and often pairing it with that lovable sidestick, sausage.

Third, whenever I'm at a baseball game and they do a pizza race on the jumbotron, I wholeheartedly and consistently root for sausage. Almighty Sausage, I will always be in your corner.

Finally, I've often been described as "sausagey" myself. Slightly chubby and with a reddish complexion often exacerbated by beer consumption, I sometimes resemble a man-sized sausage. My Czech heritage only reinforces my point. My motherland has the highest per-capita beer consumers and last time I czeched, we make a mean sausage too.

For all of the aforementioned reasons, it is apparent that I am a natural fit for being your inaugural Celebrity Sausage. I thank you for your time & look forward to your response.

Sincerely,
Eric Hodek, Hot Dog Guy

CHECK, PLEASE!

Hot Doug's is a great name for a gay bar. And when you go on TV and state that the owner of Hot Doug's is unusually friendly and has a truly unique way of handling sausages, it doesn't dispel the rumors. Such was my experience in the summer of 2005, when I went on *Check Please!* to tout Hot Doug's, my favorite encased-meats emporium. I had been a fan of Hot Doug's since its days on Roscoe and Oakley. So when a friend suggested that I submit an application to appear on WTTW's new show, Hot Doug's quickly came to mind.

Of course, *Check, Please!* has gone on to become a very popular series, but in 2005 it was brand new. In retrospect, I should have had more to drink before going on air (isn't that always good advice?). Sadly I failed to utter Doug's famous encased-meats tagline, but my fellow reviewers were both in awe of the tubular haute cuisine served up by Doug. These days it seems like every schmuck with a chef's toque is frying things in duck fat or beef tallow, but back then Doug was blazing new territory. We owe him a debt of gratitude for the current trend of artery-clogging menu items in restaurants across Chicago and the nation. And as for the staying power of Doug's simply delicious idea, the two other restaurants reviewed on that episode have long since closed.

The reward for my labors was a weeklong stint as the Celebrity Sausage, right there on the wall next to Elvis, Britney Spears, and all the other beautiful people. I'm proud to say that the Gary Lazarski was a mouthwatering ribeye steak sausage with horseradish cream sauce and roasted whole garlic cloves. It even earned a mention on a website, where someone moaned, "I should have ordered the Gary Lazarski." (A common lament.)

So hats off to Doug Sohn. His refusal to work anything other than "French hours" assures that every visit will require a wait, but it's always worth it. I love his sausage. —GARY LAZARSKI

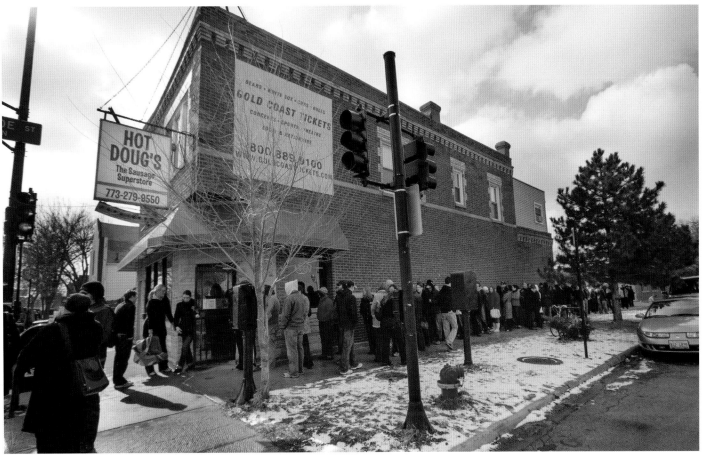

The Beginnings of the Line

From the very first day we reopened, there was a line. I had sent an email announcing our reopening and requesting that everybody please not show up all at once. People apparently missed that part.

Anyway, we were successful and profitable from the start. Our crowds at the new place were always bigger than at the old place, but the restaurant was also bigger and way more efficient. There was always a line, but not like there is now.

In October 2005, we were featured on *Check, Please!*, a show on the local PBS station (WTTW) that reviewed Chicago-area restaurants. From that point on, things skyrocketed. That was the event that genuinely changed our business.

The Line Experience

This is the one aspect of the restaurant with which I really have no firsthand experience. I basically know nothing about it. Which is nice, because I don't have to do any of the waiting. I'm going to go have a sausage now. Here's what people in line have had to say.

PHOTO BY WENDY GUNDERSON

 The new Hot Doug's opened January 4. Sohn has duplicated the goofy décor of the old place, chockablock witih Elvibilia and hot-dog-related kitsch.

Another difference is the relative desolation of the neighborhood…but Sohn sees advantages. The new place is roomier…and there's plenty of street parking. Gordon Tech is just three blocks north, and the employees of Midway Games and WMS Gaming work right across the street. If opening day was any indication, he doesn't have anything to worry about. One hour before the 4PM closing time, the line was still backed up to the door.

CHICAGO READER, JANUARY 14, 2005
(BY MIKE SULA)

HATE LINES, HATE TWITTER

I hate lines. I hate Twitter. I hate driving five minutes outside my safety bubble of the West Loop and Restaurant Row. It pisses me off when people name crappy restaurants in Chicago because they think they're in the know. There are only three places in Chicago where I'll bother to stand in line: PQM, city court so I can dispute a bogus parking ticket, and Hot Doug's. I follow you to see the updates and to get some inspiration. I never thought Hot Doug's would follow me, especially considering I have three tweets to my name.

You have great taste. It's interesting how a hot dog stand can make people sign up for a public social service just to find out what kind of encased meat it's rocking that week. I bet more people know about duck-fat Fridays than any political event in the city. Keep up the tradition, keep rocking the foie.

Every time I come in I feel like a family member. Standing in line with the "totally worth it" conversations before the amazing treat of being able to zip in makes it a unique experience. **—BRIAN JAYMONT**

NEW YORK STATE OF MIND

One fine summer afternoon, I was waiting in line with my future wife. We had been waiting about an hour, and had about an hour left to go, but we brought a crossword puzzle so we were very content to wait. The couple behind us was from New York and clearly becoming agitated. I politely turned to them and suggested that the food was well worth the wait, and that now they would have a story to tell. One of them commented, "In New York, we wouldn't tolerate this line. I could open a hot dog place across the street and make a killing." I smiled and responded, "In Chicago, we wouldn't tolerate that kind of douche-baggery. No one would eat at your hot dog place because we are willing to wait for high-quality food served by people who love this community as much as we do." They both laughed, and we got acquainted and everyone enjoyed encased meat that day. There was much rejoicing.

—DAVE SWANSON

REVERIE

He was looking dreamily toward the front of the line with his sausage fest shirt...

—NICK CALDWELL

THEY SHOULDA LISTENED

In summer of 2010, a friend and I waited in line for almost two hours for some amazing encased meats. While in line, we started chatting with the folks behind us and they told us they had driven from Wisconsin solely to eat at Doug's. They asked what to get, and being a veteran I suggested anything from the specials menu. After all, while they are damn good, you can get a hot dog anywhere, but you don't find antelope or rattlesnake sausages in any old place.

As usual my friend and I ordered six sausages to share (variety is the spice of life), while the people behind us ordered something that just shocked and appalled me—and if I had to guess, it shocked Doug as well. They ordered char dogs with ketchup only. Dear God, I can't tell you why that is so wrong on so many levels. What a waste of an experience for them, and as I experienced foodgasms from the rabbit with goat cheese, I couldn't help but feel bad. We happened to leave at the same time as these unadventurous people, who claimed that Hot Doug's wasn't as special as they had hoped. Gee, I wonder why. **—MARC HENDERSON**

TEACHING PATIENCE

We love Hot Doug's and will wait as long as it takes. We started taking our first two kids to Hot Doug's when they were infants, but our littlest didn't get a chance to go until she was one and a half. This is a picture of her waiting in line with Dad and siblings during her first trip to Hot Doug's. Always worth the wait! **—LIZ & JEFF BOWEN**

HOT DOG EXAMINER BRINGS HOT DOUG'S TO CHINA

I have a lot of great memories of Hot Doug's, both while standing in the line and while enjoying many, many, many special sausages (always with duck fat fries of course!). I started writing about hot dogs for examiner.com in 2009, and Hot Doug's quickly became one of my favorite places to write about—especially since every time I went, there was something new to try.

One of my favorite line experiences was on a chilly winter day, when we were probably about 40 minutes from placing our order. A reporter and a cameraman, from Voice of America I believe, were talking to people in line when one of my friends told them they could talk to the Chicago Hot Dog Examiner. Of course they didn't quite believe that was my job title, but they decided to ask me some questions anyway. So I talked to them about hot dogs, and explained what exactly goes on a Chicago-style hot dog (something I long ago memorized: mustard, neon green relish, chopped onions, two tomato wedges, pickle spear, sport peppers, and a dash of celery salt). When the camera was done rolling, they told me the piece was for a Chinese TV report and my voice would be dubbed over in Chinese! I'll never forget that day, standing in the line talking about hot dogs, and learning that I'd be on Chinese TV! I still get a laugh out of that.

— **ELIZABETH SANFILIPPO**

BROTHERLY LOVE

I was born and raised in Chicago. I have since moved to Minnesota, where I met my wife. It only took a couple of trips back to Chicago for my wife to learn that this is the greatest food city in the country.

So a couple of years ago, after seeing Hot Doug's on several food shows, we planned to go on our next visit to Chicago to see my brother. I had heard about the line, so we planned to go for an early lunch on a Saturday. We were so excited; we had done a thorough job of reviewing the menu and could almost taste our dogs and fries. As we headed north on California, we spotted our location and saw that there were only a few people standing outside. "Great timing," we said, congratulating one another.

As we got a closer we realized that those few people we could see were blocking our view of a line that stretched around the building and down the block.

We hesitated and looked to my brother, who was not blessed with the ability to be patient. He shrugged and said he had nothing else to do, so we decided to get in line. After a while my brother went to sit in the car and listen to the radio. My wife and I continued to visit with the other people in line. Every once in a while I would walk over to where my brother was parked to check on him. He would usually wave or just give me the thumbs-up. As time went on and we got closer to the entrance, I became a little concerned about my brother. I went to check on my brother again, and he was OUT COLD SLEEPING. I found this funny, and kind of lucky, as it bought us some more time.

I returned to the line and we eventually made it to "the promised land." We placed a big order, as we had also planned to bring back lunch for my sister-in-law and my nephew, not to mention the increased hunger we had from standing in line. On the ride home we had already put away a couple of specialty dogs and an order of fries. All told we stood in line for at least two hours. The entire experience was so worth it as the food was as outstanding as expected, and my brother's patience was even better. — **CHRIS CHINN**

THE ULTIMATE HAUTE DOG: HOT DOUG'S

Scott and I have lived in Chicago for several years (we are California transplants). Our first time partaking in the Hot Doug's experience was on a warm summer day in August 2011. Our friend Brae was visiting from California; I had created a Best of Chicago itinerary for him, which included Hot Doug's for the ultimate Chicago hot dog experience.

We were prepared for a long wait, maybe 45 minutes. It felt like waiting in line for an awesome theme-park ride. This place had become kind of a big deal and there was great anticipation in the air. So we waited. We took pictures of ourselves waiting in the famous line. We inched forward. We watched others wait. No one dropped out of the line, which snaked down the long sidewalk of a quiet tree-lined street in Avondale. There are few things in life we have waited in line so long for...we were ready to be amazed. The excitement among line-goers never waned.

A father and daughter sales team appeared under a tree and tried their hand at peddling bottled waters. Then, an ice cream truck pulled up beside us. The same ice cream truck circled our line every half-hour, having no success, not realizing he was trying to sell to the same customers. Two hours later, what we had expected to be lunch turned out to be an early dinner.

We entered the restaurant and felt like we had just won something. We were welcomed by a vibrant palette of primary colors splashed about the interior, an impressive exotic hot dog menu that took up the better part of a wall, a stuffed jackalope with some bling on it, some random framed celebrity photographs on the walls, lots of kitschy vintage hot dog memorabilia.... And to our surprise, Hot Doug himself took our order! What a cool, down-to-earth guy.

We went there knowing exactly what we wanted. We all ordered the legendary rattlesnake hot dogs, shared duck fat fries, and drank ice-cold bottles of ginger beer. Best.hot.dog.ever. Best. fries.ever. Savored every bite. The wait was totally worth it; it's part of the adventure. We left Hot Doug's in a dreamlike daze as another party took our seats to rest their legs and enjoy their encased-meat marvels.

—ELIZABETH BEELER McWHORTER

Left: Elizabeth Beeler McWhorter and Scott McWhorter; middle: Scott and Brae Irwin; right: Scott, Brae, and Elizabeth.

HOT DOUG'S

93

WHAT I LEARNED STANDING IN LINE AT HOT DOUG'S

BY TONY FITZPATRICK

The line is necessary, Bunky. Part of the ritual...the preparation. The Journey. Part of the defining communal experience that is Hot Doug's.

This is Democracy in practice; a place where the bedraggled piss-bum is equal to the Mayor...and in fact maybe a bit more desirable as a lunch companion.

I'll very patiently wait the sometimes hour plus in line at Hot Doug's. Not that I am a patient man—far from it. I beat ketchup containers because they don't pour fast enough for me.

Movies over two hours annoy the hell out of me, unless it is *Inglorious Basterds*, where they torture the fuck out of Nazis just for snicks—I can watch that shit all night.

Other restaurants? Forget it. They can kiss my pasty Irish ass if they think I will stand there like some Okie-fuck waiting to spend my money there. Not in this life, Snapper-Head.

I'm a little pampered. I'm a famous Artist. That doesn't mean much in Chicago though. To be a famous Artist in Chicago is to know that translates into this level of fame: You are exactly HALF as famous as the actors who play the Lotto Balls on Channel 9. A subculture of geeks know who you are because they hate you because you make a living...sell-out.

It does mean that you can get good tables at certain Restaurants, though—and this is Chicago—we may not be the center of all culture but goddamn, we eat good.

At Hot Doug's there is a line every day. I build it into my lunch hour; my lunch hour becomes my lunch hour and a half. And that is a good thing—because of the line.

I've stood out there when it has been 10 degrees and a 40-minute wait—and do you know how I felt about that?

Like I feel every time I get to eat at Hot Doug's...Goddamn Grateful.

Lucky.

Fortunate that I am not one of those poor shit-heads standing in line for Pink's in L.A.

Or Nathan's Famous in New York. I wouldn't feed this swill to a hill of stinkbugs.

I'd rather stuff a roadkill Dachshund wrapped in a moldy jockstrap into a poppy seed bun than eat anything masquerading as a hot dog from either of these two cities.

Hot Doug's is the best in a town that does hot dogs better than any other place on the planet.

You can believe the credo boldly emblazoned on the back of a Hot Doug's t-shirt.

"There are no finer two words in the English language than encased meats, my friend."

You're goddamn skippy there aren't.

To wait in line at Hot Doug's also avails one to the thought most people have: "Wow—I wish there were other locations."

Don't think he hasn't been offered—in fact somebody suggested an airport store.

Yeah, that is exactly what Doug Sohn wants to do every day of his life—haul ass out to O'Hare.

Trust me—he'd rather pick up hot coals with his ass cheeks. The temptation to open a chain of anything usually awakens the inner pig in any person. Not Doug—what he has is perfect, singular, and only like itself. He will not fuck with perfection—he will only burnish and refine and make that which is perfect a better perfect.

Waiting in line at this Valhalla of tube steaks gives one time to contemplate these lofty thoughts to share the encased meats experience with other right-thinking members of your community.

I've met all manner of folk in this line. My favorite line companions are those who are coming to Doug's for the first time, those who are a hair peevish about the wait—the necessary procession to make oneself worthy, is how I think of it.

I take it upon myself to straighten these people the fuck up. I tell them: "Hey, Bunky...This isn't Home Depot. Doug Sohn is an artist—there are hot dogs beyond the imagination and you should use this time to cleanse yourself of all you know of inferior hot dogs. Really, make yourself worthy, Beanbag...and quit working everyone's stick about the wait. We all wait...and with a sense of gratitude that there are still things on this planet worth waiting FOR. Capisce, D-Bag?"

This usually puts their head right... I always make sure I make eye-contact after they've taken their first bite of the Duck Sausage with foie gras. When I look at them—they nod their head... they get it.

The line defines intention and purpose.

The line is holy.

Don't go fucking with it—trust me... it works.

Tony Fitzpatrick was born in Chicago in 1958. He is still there. He is still there because nobody else on the planet can figure out how to make a decent fucking hot dog. There is only Hot Doug's and a few others, and they are all here in Chicago. And, Bunky? He's not going anywhere he can't get his perfect hot dogs. You got that, Butchie?

L.A.? No. Paris? No. New York? Please. He makes drawings, collages, and etchings. He is in a bunch of museums including the Museum of Modern Art in New York. You know, the city with the shitty hot dogs.

Line of the Times

BY **JAKE MALOOLEY** · REPRINTED WITH PERMISSION FROM *TIME OUT CHICAGO*, JULY 3–9, 2008

One very hungover man puts up with an agonizingly long Saturday wait to get his hands on Hot Doug's duck-fat fries and a frank.

12:21PM Doug Sohn, owner of the insanely popular dog emporium Hot Doug's (3324 N California Ave, 773-279-9550), is the pope of encased meats, and his hungover faithful—myself included—have come out in droves. The line is spilling out the door and snaking down Roscoe Street. Head aching, I slump into the queue about 45 people away from the counter.

12:28PM I have spotted the alpha-carnivore: a 300-pound dude toting a six-pack of beer and wearing a shirt that reads, I didn't claw my way to the top of the food chain to eat vegetables. Can't decide what's making me gag: the sight of his brews or the thought of someone having an outfit designated for meat consumption.

12:42PM People stream outside carrying Cokes and wearing smiles. One of these lucky bastards announces to no one in particular, "Color me satisfied!" The hungry mob collectively fantasizes about his demise as he crosses traffic-heavy California Avenue.

12:48PM A welcome bout of the hangover burps (you know what I'm taking about) has brought my appetite back. Like a Bugs Bunny cartoon hallucination, the elderly woman in front of me starts to look like a giant, glistening frank. I desperately attempt to bribe her with $1 for her spot in line. She refuses: "You gotta up the price, sonny!"

12:55PM My life has become a Jerry Seinfeld waiting-room joke as we're corralled into progressively smaller vestibule and staging areas. I can faintly hear things being grilled.

12:58PM I'm fuming as people ahead of me milk their face time with Doug; someone gets reprimanded by one of Doug's minions for stepping out of line to save a table. Not in his house!

1:01PM Exactly 40 minutes after the culinary quest begins, I finally make it to Doug's register and order. Doug does the math in his head, of course, totally unfazed by the pandemonium around him.

1:39PM Full and hangover-free, I exit gloatingly with my Coke and requisite smile. Color me satisfied, indeed.

A THIN LINE BETWEEN DUCK AND FATE BY "BYRON GRESTIN"

Note from contributor: This is a nonfiction short story I have written concerning a memorable line experience at Hot Doug's. All of the names have been slightly changed due to references regarding illegal substance use. We have all been to Hot Doug's on countless occasions, but this story is a recollection of by and far the most memorable of those occasions.

After a Friday evening that entailed heavy drinking, and a night poisoned by sleepless anxiousness, the three of us prepared for a Saturday that would be oversaturated with delectable duck fat fries. Like any other typical journey to Hot Doug's, Davis, Harlin, and I properly equipped ourselves for the inevitability of a tedious wait in line by smoking a copious amount of marijuana.

Of course, it was just as much our goal to make the sensory experience of eating at Hot Doug's as invigorating as possible. In addition, we thought it best to starve ourselves in anticipation of the coming meal. What better way to fully appreciate the fatty and filling foods that awaited us. Unfortunately, we would later come to realize that this may have been a cataclysmic mistake.

As we turned the corner at California and Addison, and sped down the straightaway across from ComEd, we got our first glimpse of the line. It was certainly not the longest line I had ever seen, but just about any line outside of Hot Doug's at least resembles something you would see at Six Flags Great America. About 20 or 30 individuals stretched half-way down the towering outer brick wall of the restaurant, which stood as a barricade between us and the sausages we so desperately craved.

Making our way to the back of the line,

we stared at all the nameless faces that would be devouring their precious encased meats far sooner than us. We heard the insignificant garrulous ravings of the bemused tourists, and the lingering silences of the emaciated locals among us. In between the sporadic and momentary shuffling of feet, we mindlessly stared at our phones and contemplated what we would eat. "Should I get venison or duck with foie gras?" I indecisively asked myself. "Maybe I'll try something I've never had before," I thought, when my careful rumination was abruptly cut off.

"Fuck! I forgot to bring cash," exclaimed Harlin, in a forceful and succinct manner. "I'm gonna run to an ATM real quick."

And then, as if he were cued, Davis promptly added, "Oh shit, I forgot cash too. I'll come with you."

So there I was, left alone to my own devices, as Harlin and Davis scurried off to find the closest greenback depository. "Well, I better pretend to look at my phone again," I noted, trying my best not to look too discomforted or high. But as the line started to gradually move forward, and as more hungry customers filled in behind me, the paranoia took hold.

Five minutes went by, and then 10 minutes. Finally it had been almost 15 minutes since Harlin and Davis had left, and I was

now approaching the front door of the establishment. Would they make it back in time? Would they make it back at all? "Maybe they were brutally murdered on the way to the ATM by a roving pack of vengeful ducks that had escaped from the Lincoln Park Zoo," I pondered. No one could know for sure. Perhaps this was a sign that it was simply the wrong day to go to Hot Doug's.

Finally, seemingly out of nowhere, Harlin and Davis safely returned without any duck-related injuries. It turned out that their trip to the ATM was far less harrowing than I had imagined. Furthermore, during those long and worrisome 15 or so minutes, in which I was hoping for my friends' safe return, I had in fact made a considerable amount of progress in the line. However, our perilous journey in the Hot Doug's line had only truly just begun.

For the uninitiated, the line outside of Hot Doug's may appear to be an ordinary chain of impatient gluttons at an exceedingly popular restaurant. However—similar to the structure of the film *The 36th Chamber of Shaolin*—once inside the actual doorway of the restaurant, there are a series of small compartments that patrons must navigate through in order to advance in the line. Only the strongest and most resolute restaurant patrons shall experience the glory of being a sausage master, after having passed through these chambers.

As Harlin, Davis, and myself entered the very first chamber, we were poised for battle. The room was only big enough for the three of us and a middle-aged white man with glasses who somewhat resembled Steve Allen. Through the glass window of our chamber, we could see the ebullient faces of the masses as they devoured their salivation-inducing sausages. The seductive aroma of the oily duck fat fries and the charred exotic meats acted as unsympathetic Sirens, toying with our sanity and our appetites. Right about this moment, our hunger pangs struck with irrevocable force. Silence filled the chamber, and our knees began to buckle.

Time is relative, therefore I would argue that our time spent in that first chamber of Hot Doug's was relatable to time spent at an extended family reunion—a hellish, unending torrent of uncomfortable silence and accidental eye contact followed by a feeling of utter helplessness. So as soon as Harlin and I noticed that the second, even smaller chamber had cleared out, we swung the door open and dashed inside. Initially, we were relieved at our progress but then we noticed we were missing something...Davis.

Davis was back in the first chamber, with his eyes closed, leaning up against the wall. Steve Allen was trying to nudge Davis, and urging him to move up in line. Astonishingly, Davis failed to respond. His eyes remained closed and his face was beyond pale. Perhaps it was the combination of a

sleepless night, a bad hangover, being too high, and not eating anything—but Davis had somehow managed to pass out while standing in line.

To be clear, Davis did not merely drop to the ground as you might imagine an unconscious person to do. He was actually able to remain standing while being incapacitated. Harlin and myself were mystified; we didn't know what to do. Steve Allen and the other strangers surrounding Davis were starting to get concerned. After all, it's not every day that a 6' 4" gap-toothed Polish man passes out while standing next to you in line. Consequently, Harlin and I returned to the first chamber in an attempt to revive Davis.

"Davis, wake up! We're next in line," yelled Harlin, as he tried to shake Davis out of his stupor. "C'mon man, sausages!" I added, with a few pokes to Davis's side.

At last, Davis slowly opened his bloodshot eyes and gasped for air as if he had been underwater for too long. Harlin and I hastily took a half step back to give Davis room to breathe. Our tall Polish friend looked incredibly disoriented, malnourished, and was essentially unintelligible. The crowd around us was growing increasingly worried. A kindly young woman, perhaps a school teacher or a nurse during weekdays, sensibly said, "I think I'm going to get him a glass of water..."

"It's OK. I got it," interrupted Harlin. He quickly took control of the situation and ran off to the soda fountain. In an instant, Harlin was back with a large cup of cold water for Davis.

Harlin and I asked our friend if he was alright, as he slowly drank down the water. He insisted that he was fine, and we wanted to believe him, mainly for selfish reasons. Hot Doug was just 20 feet from where we stood. Sausages and duck fat fries were just another 20 minutes away, at the most. We had come so far, and waited so long, but this unpredictable incident put our sausage fest in jeopardy. What was more important? Davis's well-being, or well-cooked sausages?

We looked at Davis, then at Doug. One more time at Davis, and again at Doug. It was one of the hardest and most painful decisions I've ever had to make, but to ensure our friend's survival, we made an about-face and exited the doors of Hot Doug's. The car ride home was mostly silent with the occasional, "Fuck! Why did we leave?" All in all, it was probably for the best. Who knows what would have happened if we stayed. Maybe those bloodthirsty ducks from the zoo would have found and killed us all.

It should be noted that the three of us have not been back to Hot Doug's as a group since this fiasco took place. However, Harlin and I did go on a solo expedition to Hot Doug's later that week. We feared that another trip with Davis might result in yet another bizarre and ill-fated incident, so we wanted to ensure safe sausage consumption. Thankfully, this time around, no one passed out and duck sausages were indeed eaten.

SAUSAGE DOUBLE ENTENDRES

1 **"How big is that sausage?"**

2 **"I've always wanted to eat my own sausage." (Said by the actual "celebrity" of the celebrity sausage.)**

3 **"Is one going to fill me up?"**

4 **"I really like your sausage." (Best when said by a handsome woman.)**

5 **Let's face it, pretty much any sentence with the word sausage in it is possibly a double entendre.**

MIDWAY'S GAME

I used to work across the street from Hot Doug's, at Midway Games. We loved stopping by to pick up lunch but the line was often a hassle. We noticed there were people who bypassed the wait and were able to pick up their food as soon as they walked in. That's when we discovered the magic of placing a phone order for pickup.

We began almost exclusively calling ahead, until one day when we were informed that phone orders now required a minimum purchase of $15. Thereafter, if someone had a craving for encased meats we would try to get as many people to go in on a phone order as possible.

We never confirmed it but we were pretty sure Midway was responsible for the new phone order minimum. It may be gone now, but Midway Games loved Hot Doug's.

—DAVID TURKIEWICZ, GHOST OF MIDWAY GAMES

PROMISE KEPT

This is the promised story of my brother's first visit to Hot Doug's. It's a bright, hot Saturday afternoon, three summers ago...

Jeanette and I have promised Michael a trip to Hot Doug's. He loves a good hot dog as much as anyone, loves sausage, loves nearly anything that fits in a hot dog bun.

The line is shockingly long by the time we arrive. We stand west of the WMS satellite office, if you can believe that. An opportunistic Good Humor truck is parked on Roscoe especially for us. And he's barraged! We figure he's done a couple thousand in business—mostly ice pops and water bottles—by the time he drives away, having run out of change. In a gesture of goodwill, one of Hot Doug's staff people comes out with a hot dog and fries for this Good Humor fellow who kept your hottest, thirstiest customers from slinking away. Some folks ahead of us claim the dog, and the fries are passed up the line. Most everyone grabs a couple.

The group ahead of us has some punk-rock types, two of whom drive off in search of beer. The beer questers return with a 30-pack, and each of their group opens one. After that, the beer enterprise begins in earnest, and several people pony up a dollar for a cold one. One of the punk rockers is kind enough to notice that Jeanette is looking a trifle heat-exhausted, and offers her a beer gratis.

Sometimes a free can of cheap beer from a chick with multiple piercings reminds us why we love Chicago. I think she may have taken a shining to Jeanette ;-)

At this point, we've been in line nearly two hours and we're still staring at a number of folks in front. If not for the promise we'd made to Michael, Jeanette and I wouldn't consider waiting this long. Hell, we wouldn't consider getting in line where we did. But now we've lost much of the afternoon and we're starving and committed to the endeavor. We're all in, as they say.

Once we get in and sit down, we look at our watches. Two hours and 45 minutes have passed since we got in line. Two hours, 45 minutes. The duration of a baseball game. The length of a long, satisfying nap. The time it takes to drive to Saugatuck, Michigan. The time it takes to fly to Las Vegas.

And yet, no regrets. A promise kept. And encased meats enjoyed, finally. **—ALEC ROSS**

UNCLE TIME

I was first taken by one of my older cousins to Hot Doug's, in 2009. It was a Saturday morning. Not knowing what to expect, (my concept of a "long line" would change after several more visits), we showed up 15 minutes before the place opened. As we made our way through, inch by inch, foot by foot, we made acquaintances with the others in line, and shared random stories and updates about life and the world at large. Suffice to say, the wait felt shorter than the 30 minutes we were actually in it. Finally getting to the register and checking the menu out, I was blown away. Up to this point, I did not know so many things could go on a bun and into a hot dog.

This past year I started taking my niece and nephew. They know that when I show up at their house, I'm going to take them someplace cool. Usually, if it's a Saturday morning, it's Hot Doug's. Saturday mornings we know when to show up and snipe an early spot in line. It's a good start to the weekend. We've waited on freezing winter days and on hot, hot days in the summer. Each time, it's worth it. It's memorable. It's fun. I hope Hot Doug's is open long enough for my niece and nephew to start taking my (future) kids one day. It gives me a nice excuse to hang out and take them to a place they recognize and remember. I take them to a lot of new places and things, like movies, restaurants, and shows, but Hot Doug's has always been a consistent spot where we can expect a good time and good food. And while a familiar spot, it always has a feeling of being refreshing and new. Being able to share that little bit of time and happiness with them means a lot to me, and I'm glad to have Hot Doug's be a part of it.

—MARTIN ARAGO

CHAPTER 5

Inside Hot Doug's: The Vibe

The Look

For me to feel comfortable at the restaurant and have the necessary energy and focus, the place had to be somewhere that I wanted to go every day. So my choices in music, furniture, decoration, even the names of the sausages, are all things that I really like and find inspirational.

Elvis

I'm a huge fan of rock and pop music, except for the Grateful Dead, jam bands, and improvisational jazz. I consider the three-minute pop song to be one of the greatest achievements there is. Growing up, there were five radio stations and three of them played Elvis, so of course I was familiar with his music. When my friend Don moved from Chicago to San Diego, he asked me to join him for the drive, which required a

stop in southern Illinois. I told him I'd go with, but only if we went to Graceland—it's on the way. This was the end of summer, 1986. Graceland hadn't been open for too long. For some reason, I had a compelling need to stop there. I was a fan, but not a huge fan.

Going to Graceland wasn't a total epiphany, but I was mesmerized. I realized that this is the guy. He strongly influenced Dylan and Lennon and countless others. The whole cultural phenomenon around him, the devotion of his fans, and the fact that people dress up as him and then stand in line for hours at Graceland made me gain a newfound respect for him. I didn't really realize what this guy meant to so many people until I went there and saw for myself the hysteria that he caused.

I began making trips every year to see Graceland. I think I did it 12 years in a row. Through this annual trip, I learned about his life and his music and I became fascinated. (It's a great road trip too, good food along the way, and every time it's different.)

For me, there's a religious aspect to it. I'm still a huge fan of his music—he was hugely talented. He's such an iconic figure. Pure human emotions are derived from him. And yet he's just a guy. One guy.

Madonna

I'm a big fan of Madonna, always have been. I find her inspiring—both her music and who she is as a pop-culture phenomenon. But mostly, she's someone who does what she wants to do, and she has been very successful at it. She works in an industry where you need to generate sales and appease customers, and she calls the shots and does things on her terms. I find that truly admirable. Plus she's a fabulous babe.

She has been doing her thing for a really long time in an arena that tends not to favor longevity. One could say the same about restaurants. Possibly.

Wall of Fame

As I have mentioned, we use the word "celebrity" very loosely at Hot Doug's. We have created a wall of celebrity photos, appropriately enough, in the bathroom foyer. Numerous celebrities have sent or dropped off autographed photos. Not to exclude anyone, but I do have a few favorites. In no particular order:

1. MARTY ALLEN: A friend of Marty Allen's called me and said that Marty was thrilled to have his name on the menu and gave me his address to request an autograph. Receiving his photo in the mail was truly a great thrill. Especially since I used to be a diesel fitter. I worked in a woman's underwear factory where I would hold them up and say, "diesel fitter."

2. THE MILWAUKEE BREWER RACING SAUSAGES: The most exciting minute and a half in all of sports.

3. SHARON STONE: Well, it's not really a signed photo of Sharon Stone. It's a picture of my dad stalking Sharon Stone, and he signed it.

Hot Doug's is the place I go when I call in sick. One of my favorite things is the weird fish-eye mirror. This is a self-portrait I took in it. See you on my next sick day! — **TIM PIGOTT**

4. JOE DeVIVO: Coauthor Kate DeVivo's dad. It's not really a favorite, but Kate is very nice and I thought she might like this.

5. JAMES CAAN: It's actually a photo of James Caan holding a copy of our CD, "Theme from Hot Doug's." It's Sonny Corleone, for Pete's sake!!

6. PAMELA ANDERSON: It's not actually her signature. It's signed by the author of the book that Pam is reading, Anne Elizabeth Moore.

7. LARRY GRENNAN: The real name of famed Chicago new wave artist Wazmo Nariz. A customer brought Wazmo's dad into the restaurant a few years ago and Waz sent me this letter, his second album, and a couple of "I ♥ Wazmo" bumper stickers. Receiving this was a genuine thrill. I'm a huge fan and I've got my high school yearbook to prove it.

WALL OF FAMER: MATT ROAN

I have been going to Hot Doug's at least monthly for the last five years. Being a regular guest, I became friendlier with Doug each time I came in. We typically talk about Chicago sports, music, and how my love of the merguez lamb sausage with harissa and goat cheese rivals my love for my own mother.

So, just about a year back, I show up to the desk to order and Doug won't talk to me. I'm confused. He dips under his desk to reveal a copy of *Time Out Chicago* that featured me on the cover. He hands it over, gives me a Sharpie and says, "Sign it. You're going up on the Wall of Fame." I was in shock! I had finally arrived. It was all so wild to me that all I could muster was a crappy "To: Doug, From: Matt Roan."

I'm hoping this story makes the book so I can give you the proper thanks you deserve Doug. It's seriously a crazy honor to be on the Wall of Fame and I feel as if I've made it as a Chicagoan, an eater, and a man.

—**DJ MATT ROAN**

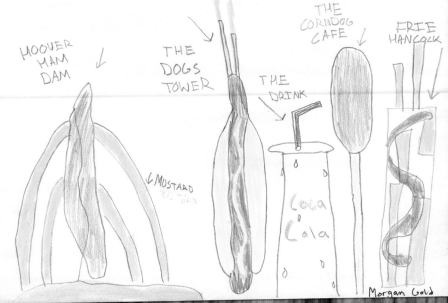

OUR DREAM CHICAGO

HOOVER MAM DAM

THE DOGS TOWER

THE DRINK

THE CORNDOG CAFE

ERIE HANCOCK

↓MUSTARD

Coca Cola

Morgan Gold

My dream Chicago features a city filled with nothing but supermodels and championship sports teams, but this rendition from a customer is nice, too.

Red Hot Annie

Our Facebook cover photo contest winner (which I knew nothing about).

BUTTON-O-MATIC OF THE YEAR
HOT DOUGS
2011

2011
GOLDEN
BUTTON
AWARD
WINNER

I've received a number of awards; this is one of them.

Me, if I haven't had my morning bourbon.

My man Gus on Halloween. Truth be told, he's not the first person to dress up as me for Halloween, but he's definitely the best looking.

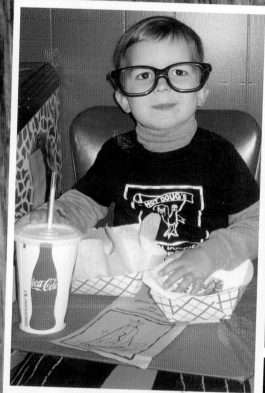

CRITICAL LINKS: A HISTORY OF ENCASED MEATS BY HUGH MUSICK

Primitive Utensils (recreated here) suggest that encased meats played a vital role in Neanderthal life.

Trojan Wiener Ancient Greek legend recounts how Odysseus played upon King Priam's weakness for encased meats to gain entry into his heavily fortified city. The Trojan Wiener was rolled to the gates of the fortress and presented as a peace offering. Warriors hidden inside quickly gained control of the city and won the war.

400 B.C.

486 A.D.

Clovis, King of the Franks Clovis drives the Romans from Soissons in northern Gaul in 486 A.D. During Roman occupation all encased meats were sent to Rome as a form of taxation, never to be tasted by northern Europeans. Upon liberating the city, Clovis made the humble "frankish" sausage, also known as the "frank," available to all men.

200,000 B.C.

600 B.C.

1100 A.D.

Cave Paintings from Lascaux, France, provide the first concrete evidence that Ice Age Man knew how to convert bison into delicious Mountain Man sausage.

Thucydides Spanikopita accidentally substitutes pork for lamb in his sausage recipe. The result is a stunning development. He begins hawking his polis sausage in front of the Acropolis. Over time, Athenians slur the words together and it soon becomes known as the Polish.

Charlemagne, King of Franks Credited with introducing yellow mustard to the world. Also, Charlemagne demanded all sausages made in the Frankish Kingdom measure at least as long as his foot, thus giving rise to the foot-long dog.

One of the things I've gotten better at (I said better, not good) is delegating. Especially delegating things I don't do well. So, when a friend now asks, "Is there anything I can do to help?" my new response is, "Heck yeah, what've you got in mind?" Friend and artist Hugh Musick suggested a hot dog history timeline. I

Botticelli's Birth of a Chili Dog Scholars agree that the resurgence of art and culture in Europe in the 1400s is entirely attributable to the discovery of the chili dog.

1420 A.D.

1789 A.D.

Vive les Saucissons! Fed up with difficult-to-carry rich foods in elaborate cream sauces, the French rose up against the aristocracy, demanding eminently toteable sausages.

Houston, We Have Sausage NASA launches an ambitious plan to put a hot dog cart on the moon. Technical problems arising from the impenetrable barrier of an astronaut's helmet resulted in the program being scrapped the following year. Scientists hope to restart the effort on the international space station in 2010.

1973 A.D.

1542 A.D.

1916 A.D.

1990 A.D.

Anatomy of a Thuringer The Age of Science saw tremendous advances in the study of the human body, with perhaps the most important being the discovery of encased meats' vital role in human longevity.

Send a Salami to Your Boy in the Army! Fueled by sausage, the American fighting machine grew strong and unstoppable. Even the elite German Knockwurst regiment, armed with their newly created "Kaiser" rolls, was no match for American encased-meats might.

Encased Meats Enter the Nuclear Age Advances in small particle physics, coupled with Americans' demands for increasingly spicy foods, led the Atomic Energy Commission in 1990 to begin work on a super hot Atomic Dog. This highly controversial sausage is not yet available to the public.

told him I had a blank wall that was all his. The result, Critical Links: A History of Encased Meats, is now legendary. By the way, it took an 11-year-old son of a customer to point out the fact that the BC portion of the timeline is incorrect. Good thing I was never an editor...oh, wait.

PHOTOS BY ROYA JADE

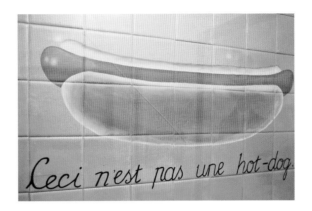

Ceci n'est pas une hot-dog.

The Murals

My friend Louise Baker moved back to Chicago from Florida a year or so after we reopened the new store. (She is now Louise Ahrendt—she got married in Napa a couple of years ago. When she asked me if I attended because it was her wedding or because it was in Napa, I had to honestly reply, "Well, if you got married in Omaha, I wouldn't have closed the store.") She is a muralist, and she asked me if I knew anyone who needed anything, well, muraled.

I thought about this for a bit and told her that I hoped she wouldn't be offended, but I'd always wanted to do something to the bathrooms. Apparently, she didn't take offense at all. We talked over a few ideas and I told her that my favorite painter was René Magritte. She did a remarkable job. The *American Gothic* parody in the women's bathroom was her idea (a damned good one). *Ceci n'est pas une hot-dog* is in the men's room. This has to be some of the greatest bathroom art in a hot dog stand that was ever created.

THE MAKING OF "DOUG GOTHIC," "SON OF DOUG," AND "THIS IS NOT A SAUSAGE" MURALS

BY LOUISE (BAKER) AHRENDT

I lived down the street from the original Hot Doug's, then moved away from Chicago for a couple of years. When I moved back, I stopped in to say hello to Doug in his new location. I told him I had hoped he would have a blank wall for me to paint a mural, but saw they were all full. Doug replied that he had been "wanting to do something with the bathrooms."

We realized that we both enjoy the work of the artist René Magritte, so I chose a few of his iconic pieces that people would recognize. Then I thought of a few other ideas, but Grant Wood's *American Gothic* came to mind since it is a classic Chicago/Midwest image. I did not want to just repaint the artwork as is, I wanted to have murals that would reflect Doug's great sense of humor and, of course, include a hot dog theme too.

Once I had the ideas and pencil sketches worked out, I was ready to begin the painting. This was a unique project for me, though, since my "canvases" were only available when Hot Doug's was closed: each Saturday afternoon after closing, then all day Sunday. I realized that the

hardest part of working in Hot Doug's when it was closed was that I would always start to crave hot dogs! Also, it was sad to have to tell people knocking on the windows that the sausage emporium was closed and I was not able to make them any hot dogs.

It took me a few months painting on the weekends to complete the work, and when the murals were finished, I decided they needed to be properly displayed, like in a gallery, so I hand-made wood frames and attached them to the tile walls. Doug liked the idea and had an official "gallery" opening for me. I sent out announcements and Doug opened the bathrooms all day and even had cookies for the customers.

Whenever I stop by Hot Doug's, it feels good to have customers compliment the murals. I also see photos that customers have taken posted on websites.

These murals are the first of many projects I have created with Doug. He has said that he is the "Medici of Avondale," but for me, he is my best patron and friend.

Other projects I created with Doug include the fiberglass Piggies (they are grazing in the restaurant's backyard) and a "Flying Pig" sculpture. They were both created as a fundraising project with Rainbow Hospice in Park Ridge.

MENU

FRENCH-CUT FRENCH FRIES
small $1.50
large $2.25

CHEESE FRIES
small $2.25
large $3.00

DUCK FAT FRIES $3.50
(Friday & Saturday only)

HOW DO YOU LIKE YOUR SAUSAGE?
- char grilled
- deep fried
- steamed
- fried & grilled

Would You Like to Add....
CHILI: 50¢   CHEESE: 25¢

WHAT DO YOU WANT ON IT?
"Everything" means:
- tomatoes
- pickle
- celery salt
- caramelized onions

We also have:
- sport peppers
- ketchup
- raw onions
- sauerkraut
- giardiniera

Today's Specials

Smoked Texas Pork Hot Link
with Coca-Cola BBQ Sauce and Cheddar-Jack Cheese

Curry Pork and Veal Sausage
with Spinach Raita and Apple-Cinnamon Cheddar Cheese

Jalapeño-Cheddar Pork Sausage
with Mole à la Carlos and Salsa-Jack Cheese

Foie Gras and Sauternes Duck Sausage
with Truffle Aioli, Foie Gras Mousse and Fleur de Sel

Chicken Cordon Bleu Sausage
with Dijon Shallot Hot Sauce, Hickory Smoked Swiss Cheese and Fried Prosciutto

Turducken Sausage
with Pumpkin Cream and Cranberry-Infused Brûlat Sauce in Cheese

Chive and Pork Bockwurst
with Onion Dijonnaise and Truffle Affinois Cheese

One-Third Pound Spicy Cajun Heritage Pork Sausage
with Creole Mustard and Cheese-Stuffed Hot Peppers

Cognac, Lamb and Pork Sausage
with Mint Mustard Cream and Double Crème Brie Cheese

Jack Daniels and Fennel Smoked Pork Sausage
with Sage Mustard, Carrigaline Farmhouse Cheese and Crispy Fried Onions

The Dog
Chicago-Style Hot Dog with all the trimmings 'nuff said.
$2.00

The Norm Crosby
Thuringer: I represent that beef, pork, and garlic.
$3.50

The Elvis
Polish Sausage: Smoked and savory-just like the King.
$3.00

The Joe Strummer
Vegetarian Dog: Meatless... and delicious!
$3.00

The Paul Kelly
Bratwurst: Soaked in beer, sort of like Paul.
$3.50

The Steve Swisher
Chicken Sausage: Classic Italian-style or zesty Santa Fe-style.
$3.50

The Sal Greco
Italian Sausage: It's not personal, it's strictly sausage.
$3.50

The Charlie and James Sohn
Mini bagel dogs and tater tots, the kids love 'em.
$3.00

The Anna Kendrick
Fire Dog: Mighty hot!
$3.00

The Dave Pound
$3.50

The Brigitte Bardot
Andouille Sausage: Mighty, mighty, mighty hot!
$4.00

ALL PRICES INCLUDE TAX

GAME OF THE WEEK

Mark Bello is the chef/owner of Pizza a Casa Pizza School in New York City. While Mark is not a legendary comedian, he is still pretty damn funny and one day expects Doug will bestow him the appropriate props and name the Thuringer after him.

CHAIRS, MENUS, AND WIENER SIGNS BY MARK BELLO

I am proud to call myself an early adopter of Hot Doug's, back in the day when he was first on Roscoe. I was somewhat of a regular, workday permitting and assuming I could time visits strategically around the lunch hour(s) of the nearby high school kids who monopolized his tables and threw french fries at each other. Please understand, I am not judging, I was that high school kid too and I pity those in my past who had to endure my obnoxiousness. But I digress…

My "collaboration" with Hot Doug began when I would show up on a Friday afternoon (late but not so late as to be insensitive to closing time—bravo for Doug for

sticking to the hours he has always kept). I would show up "strategically/considerately" late with homemade aioli (a.k.a garlic mayo) in tow plus a tablecloth, a bottle o' vino, and a candle (cause that's how I roll), ready to order some duck fat fries and a sausage or two that Doug recommended. We would start talking. I would give Doug aioli. We became friends.

I own a furniture store. Doug needed furniture. We bartered sausages for sofa sleepers. Then I moved to Italy for three months to pursue my passion for food, not furniture. During my stay in Italy, when Europeans and other travelers would ask me what I missed most about Chicago, I would say,

"Gimlets at the Matchbox and Thuringers at Hot Doug's."

I was saddened to hear the news that Hot Doug's was shuttered due to a fire. So upon my return I contacted Doug to express my condolences and we went out to lunch. As Doug and I walked on Lincoln Avenue, a car, actually multiple cars, drove by and said "Yo Doug—when you gonna reopen?!?" Hot dog paparazzi were not far behind. Doug expressed to me that he had had a great run and was content with his success; he was OK ending on a high note, as in "better to burn out than to fade away" (but not exactly like that because he'd more likely quote something more punk rock but with the same sentiment).

GAME OF THE WEEK

MOUNTAIN MAN Sausage
(a damn tasty combination of Elk, Antelope, Buffalo and Venison)
with Sweet Peppadew Dijonnaise and St. Nectaire Cheese
$8.50

CELEBRITY SAUSAGE

LINCOLN KILPATRICK

SAUCISSE DE TOULOUSE
w/ GARLI
& TERR

A PERFECT EXAMPLE OF OUR LIBERAL USE OF THE WORD "CELEBRITY." LINCOLN KILPATRICK WAS ONE OF THE SIX ACTORS WE USED THAT WEEK WHO STARRED IN THE 1970S MASTERPIECE, SOYLENT GREEN. BUT PLEASE NOTE: THERE IS ABSOLUTELY NO CONNECTION BETWEEN SOYLENT GREEN AND HOT DOUG'S SAUSAGES.

Thankfully, it turned out he was not actually ready to stop rocking and rolling on a poppy seed bun.

Flash forward: Doug discovers his new space. The shop is also on Roscoe, but far enough away from the french fry–throwing high school hordes and right across from the pinball/now digital slot machine–making, encased meat–loving Chicago industrial parks and destined to be an inter-

national destination for supreme sausage seekers around the globe.

With a new spot to trick out, Doug needed furniture and design. So in addition to futons, I was in the business of barstools and diner chairs, and Doug and I had some fun putting together the multi-colored red/yellow/blue chairs and stools you sit on at his spot. My furniture store is known for "quirky" window displays—and that's what I figure got me the job designing Doug's menu boards (plus my mantra, "Will do design for encased meat" probably helped, too). If you've been to Hot Doug's in the last seven years or so, you've seen my work and ordered off of it.

I'm proud of the "Celebrity Sausage" sign and the "Game of the Week" sign, but I would have to say my favorite creation (and collaboration) with Doug is in the bathroom area. Originally, Doug expressed to me the idea of a men's room sign saying "Wieners" and a ladies' room saying "No Wieners." Funny as it was, I regard Doug as a classy guy and feared his "f' 'em if they can't take a joke" idea would instigate many uncomfortable and off-putting parent/child talks from otherwise lovely customers. We ended up creating these signs.

THE MUSTARD'S GUSTO BY RICK NEUHAUS

There is a hot dog man situated rather nicely on California Avenue
He serves up soft drinks, exotic sausages and a nice slice of subtle attitude.
He's got duck-fat fries, temporarily or barely illegal fois gras,
Raw onions, mustard, relish, but no clear sign of the dreaded cole slaw.
Why don't YOU make the call . . .
Will it be steamed, char-grilled or fried?
When it comes t'some of your most popular comfort foods
I guess you could say . . . full-fat . . . has now officially arrived.
Oh, there's a little chicken sausage this . . . and a soy dog that,
But the natives are there to eat kinda heavy
And most likely and most rightly . . . enjoy a nice light chat.

HEY!
Rhymed lines can go all boring, as you may notice on this day.
It's all good ole America the Wonderful and Americana the Great.
Ain't it kinda like the 1950s with a fair portion of midwestern gourmet.
Put on your comfort clothes and map-quest most directly your own way.
SAY-HEY!
You and yours have never been there . . . and yet let's say
Still believe you have a decent respect for common good taste.
Were you born to live a meaty life or just encased,
Do you persist to insist on playing it all a lil' too safe?
Boy, do I now have a hot doggie-style suggestion to play
Beyond that, what d'folk do you expect any of us to say?
YAY-HEY!
You had better ketchup and go for the mustard's gusto
And just exactly where you are . . . do – not – the hell stay!
The heated treats are served up hot from the Doug-out.
Just look at all the hungry batters lined up smiling
Around the corner from the warm . . . home plate.
In addition, you had better swing-batter-swing because anything
Beyond 4 pm . . . is already . . . waaaaay too late.
OH and maybe one more HEY! . . . did I forget to mention
That the entire ordeal . . . is Always . . . and Totally . . .
Worth the eff'n wait!
You are all now invited to resume your relentless quest for the perfect mate!

HIGH MARKS IN MIKE'S HOT DOG CLUB

I love this place. One of my favorite eating establishments in all of the city. I may not be one of the veterans or regulars that's been coming to Hot Doug's since his first hot dog stand, but I've been coming to his Sausage Superstore every Monday for the past six months or so. I'm grateful for my friend Kay for telling me about this place.

I'm a born and raised Chicagoan, so pizza and hot dogs are two of my favorite culinary foods. I am also a loyalist. I used to go to this hot dog stand in the suburbs religiously. Which means once I find a place, I usually stick with it. I entered Hot Doug's for the first time in June 2011. Skeptical at first, with the line and all. Saw Doug Sohn taking the orders, and when it was my time in front, I told him this was my first time here, and I'm usually a very loyal hot dog eater so I rarely try new hot dog stands. He thanked me for that and I ordered two hot dogs with all the trimmings and took it to go.

The best things about what makes Hot Doug's the best hot dog stand in Chicago are the food (upscale fast food is what
I like to call it), the atmosphere when you eat in, and the friendly service that starts with Doug. Honest, down to earth, easy to talk to. He's real. Genuine. You can't hide that, even if you tried. We Chicagoans know an act, and Doug truly loves what he does, and it shows when he talks to the customers. And it filters down to all of the hard workers. Nice people that really want your experience to be an enjoyable one, no matter if it's your first time or 100th time.

I'm happy to say that Hot Doug's is my first choice for a great classic, Chicago-style hot dog with all the freshly prepared trimmings. Keep doing what you do Mr. Sohn, and I'll be there every Monday with a smile on my face.

—**MICHAEL VILLAMIN** (or how Doug takes the name of my order… **"MIKE V"**)

The Music

One of the best things about my job is that I get to listen to my records all day, every day. For you youngsters out there, when I say "records," I of course mean "CDs," or I guess I mean "my iPod machine." I like to think that I have a pretty wide range of taste when it comes to music, as long as it's a three-minute pop song that was preferably recorded sometime between 1974 and 1988.

So, if you dine at Hot Doug's, you're going to hear a lot of Buzzcocks, the Clash, Devo, the B-52s, Elvis Costello, Talking Heads, the Ramones, any '70s one-hit wonders ("Hooked on a Feeling," "Play That Funky Music," "Hocus Pocus" by Focus, you get the gist), a lot of '80s new wave (Duran Duran, Human League, Cyndi Lauper, XTC, et al.), personal guilty pleasures (Steve Miller Band, Madonna, Spice Girls, Britney Spears), and pretty much any song as long as it's catchy and a toe-tapper.

According to my iPod, the top five most-played songs at Hot Doug's are:

1. **"Checking Out the Checkout Girl"** — WAZMO NARIZ

2. **"Ballroom Blitz"** — SWEET

3. **"Ca Plane Pour Moi"** — PLASTIC BERTRAND

4. **"Renee Remains the Same"** — MATERIAL ISSUE

5. **"Boredom"** — THE BUZZCOCKS

I guarantee that my staff would agree that these songs are absolutely played a lot. (They may even say too much, but I disagree. And it's my store, so there.)

A customer once asked me which I dislike more: the Grateful Dead or jazz. I'm still thinking about that one.

THE OFFICIAL THEME FROM HOT DOUG'S

BY NICK MARKOS

I've known Doug since before he was "Hot."

Doug is the best friend I could ask for, and when he started the restaurant, I was excited for him and wanted to do something that would help, or at least would show some support. So, I thought I'd write and record an official theme song for him, thinking he might need to, you know, advertise or something.

The idea started with the title, a play on all those '70s movie theme songs, ("The Theme from Mahogany," "The Theme from Love Story," etc.); I thought the mock pretentiousness of the title "The Theme From Hot Doug's" would be particularly funny when paired with a very short, simple pop song. Doug and I had really met through music (at the end of college, I joined a band managed by his brother, Andy), and throughout the years we have had numerous lengthy discussions and debates about music, so I'm pretty familiar with his tastes. Whilst toying with how

to rip off a Steve Miller Band song, I decided to shift gears and go with the next-best thing (for Doug): pop/punk music. Knowing his affinity for the Ramones, the Clash, and Elvis Costello, as well as newer (at the time) bands like the Strokes, I decided to cook up an up-tempo, simple (and short) song in a similar vein, with a bit of a lo-fi sound and direct lyrics.

So, I sat down with my guitar and my notebook and started knocking around some chords. I had the Ramones' "I Wanna Be Sedated" in mind as I played with simple lyric ideas, and I wanted to work in Robbie's "encased meats" phrase. On the original recording, the verses alternated between, "I wanna eat at Hot Doug's," and, "I wanna eat a hot dog," but I eventually ditched the latter, just repeating the first line four times in a row—maximum simplicity. Then, to set up the last section of the song, I adapted a phrase my friend Alan Paterson would use when proposing an outing to Hot Doug's— he'd say things like, "Let's Doug's it up today for lunch!" (classic APat phraseology).

Musically, I went for some simple, catchy riffs, and that rhythmic clapping-and-shouting bit, which seemed to have a Ramones vibe. I put a fuzzy guitar lead on top, to spice it up like sport peppers on a dog. In the closing section, all the musical/lyrical motifs are layered on top of each other: The Ramones-style rhythmic clapping/shout of the intro-duction, the "Doug's it up" phrase, and the verse melody, "I wanna eat at Hot Doug's."

The reaction? Doug seemed to like it, which is what matters to me. As far as a wider reaction goes, it was pretty much utter silence (routine for my records), though I have met people in line at the restaurant who know the song (the clapping/shout-ing part, anyway). It has been quite popular at my live shows (including a one-time afternoon gig at the original Hot Doug's location), likely due to the fact that our friend B.A. would dress up in the hot-dog costume and dance around and sing—a role reprised by Scott Robbin when we appeared with Doug at the live show we did with Guy Fieri (that's a whole other story, involving the costume's demise). Doug even played tambourine on the song at one of my recent gigs. Doug and I have always donated any proceeds (such as they are) to charity (Intonation Music Workshop and others), so though I originally thought the restaurant would need help, it turns out that the restaurant has given way more help than it ever needed.

As I look at this little stream of consciousness, I realize that this discussion of the song is so longwinded that it will probably take way longer to read this than to actually listen to the song. So, maybe just skip this section, give the song a spin, and have an extra 4 minutes and 21 seconds back in your life.

DOUG'S NOTE:

YES, I OPENED FOR GUY FIERI. AND IT WAS ON THE SAME STAGE I ONCE SAW BRUCE SPRINGSTEEN (TRUST ME, I WOULD FEEL RIPPED OFF, TOO). IT WAS A SOMEWHAT SURREAL EXPERIENCE. THERE WAS A GREAT DEAL OF APPLAUSE AND HOOPLA. NOT FOR ME, BUT FOR CONDIMENTS. I'M NOT KIDDING. I WAS PUTTING TOGETHER A CHICAGO-STYLE HOT DOG, AND EACH TIME I WOULD MENTION WHAT I WAS PUTTING ON THE DOG (MUSTARD, RELISH, ETC.), A SIZABLE CHEER WOULD EMANATE FROM THE AUDIENCE. I CAN ONLY HOPE TO ONE DAY BE AS POPULAR AS CELERY SALT.

Above: Rocking out "The Theme from Hot Doug's" live: Scott Robbin, George Kalantzis, B.A. Rosenblum (in hot-dog suit), Matthew "Monkey" Payne, Nick Markos. (PHOTO BY ALAN PATERSON)

Right: Teaching the audience to clap and shout, "Hot Doug's!" live at the Rosemont Theatre: Scott Robbin (in hot-dog suit) and Nick Markos. (PHOTO BY TONY BIANCHI AND AMBER GRIBBEN)

The Theme From Hot Doug's

bee

**e From Hot Doug's
bee**

new rock mix: 01
acoustic mix: 02
tight mix: 03

[small print partially legible]

written by Nicholas Markos.
℗ and publishing 2011 and 2004 Nicholas Markos.

The "Official Theme from Hot Doug's" is exactly what I like: super short, super catchy, total Ramones-esque beat, catchy guitar riff, easy lyrics. My favorite: "I want the feel, I want the taste, I want the meats that are encased." So Nick did the first version of it, and then he started playing around and doing different mixes of it. There's an electro version, and one where he mixes U2's "Vertigo"; there might be nine or 10 different mixes now. He put out a CD with four of the mixes on it. We sold a bunch at the store and then started doing it for charity. He still plays it during every Christmas show. I don't think Superdawg has its own theme song. I'm not sure Charlie Trotter has one either.

There are a couple of other songs that are about or that make mention of Hot Doug's. The Budget Girls have a song that's super catchy, short, and with girl singers, of course. (That's the one thing that the "Official Theme from Hot Doug's" does not have going for it.) It was totally unsolicited and I love it. There is a Swedish jazz band that made a song called "Hot Doug's." It's, um, not my taste. There's a rap song, I hear. And apparently this song, "Maybe You Should Keep On Driving."

"MAYBE YOU SHOULD KEEP ON DRIVING"

This is a song our band wrote that involves an experience at Hot Doug's in 2009.

— JABBERJOSH

*Going down the road in Eddie Power
Gone three days without a shower
Man, I wish you all were in our shoes
At Hot Sauce Williams we ate barbecue
Hot Doug's, was that a line
Easy on the wallet, if you are ever in a bind*

*And we stood in line for an hour
and fifteen minutes
But it was worth it
And this guy stopped his car right in front of a bus
And this is what he said
"How many hot dogs are y'all gonna buy?"
I can't deny it's a good question
But at the time, Kevin Ware said what was on
everybody's mind*

*"Maybe you should keep on driving"
And not cause a wreck, so stop being a prick
I've said it all
Way to drop the ball
That is no way to go
Is it always that way because I seriously laughed
for days*

*Going back down the road, East Coast or bust
Give me a burger and fries
Oh, this tonight will be mine
Shit! Late for the show, we need to take these to go
I've said it all and I still laugh for days
Nothing is in our way
Still laughing for days
There is another old asshole sitting in the lobby
of a White Castle*

THE MYSTERIOUS HEAT OF HOT DOUG BY RICK NEUHAUS

Oh, it's a cult all right! Maybe not our parents' sinister version, but make no mistake...it has all the magnetic qualities of a cult. At least it's ours and like all proper cults, it has its charismatic leader. As loyal followers, we're each seeking a deeper connection, perhaps looking to fill a void that can't be contained in our work-a-day lunch breaks. Yes, I tend to exaggerate. But, consider that we stand in line no matter the weather, each trusting that this simple sacrifice will soon reward us with our cherished face-to-face encounter with our chosen guru of "encased" comforts. When that Zen moment finally unfolds in all of its understated glory, typically followed by a quick stop at the carbonation station and an eagle-eyed search for an open table, there's a true sense of not only accomplishment, but also a very specific hope for our immediate future. Could this be the essence of American individualism and authentic patriotism? Don't ask me; I'm more of a "it's all one big-ass planet" kind of guy. But, something definite and significant beyond a tasty lunch is going on.

Some questions are meant more for the asking than the answering. For instance, how does he pull it off? Have you ever put yourself in his mischievous shoes? In short, what's his deal? What were the special childhood influences that shaped the man at the eye of this sausage storm? What must it take to throw oneself into that sacred space between the general public's hungry desires and their ultimate satisfaction? How many of us could withstand the rigors of greeting an ongoing cast of generally dysfunctional characters that were each impacted in some small way by a strange combination, including, but not limited to, the tabs of orange sunshine circulating throughout the synaptic connections at the original Woodstock concert and the unique and ongoing social awakening that began to accelerate during the Cheney/Bush years? Perhaps I overstate the obvious when I draw our attention to this possibility. In the end, it wouldn't surprise me if this particularly charming guru was born of nature and any haphazard nurturing that may have taken place simply added context to a mission.

All things considered, Hot Doug seems content to consider himself just one of us. In addition to the quirky burdens of his guru-ship, it is also the hallowed ground of historical Americana that he rolls out on a daily basis. We each tithe appropriately to the cause, as we order from the assortment of refinements that only his culinary vision could offer up. Don't these tasty opportunities represent the simple pleasures that connect one day with the next? For example, the reassurance that I feel after finding a reputable hookup that reconnects me with my childhood memories of homemade french fries, or that post-pubescent moment when I graduated from my childhood relationship with ketchup into preferring the more adult hot dog dressings of mustard and relish. Other followers seem equally preoccupied with the homeboy joys of his exotic sausage preparations. I'm going to go out on a limb and suggest that his regular and/or duck fat fries are a universal force to be reckoned with.

The exact beginnings of this cult remain vague, but I fondly remember the specifics of my own initiation. It was a couple of years before the Roscoe fire. For seemingly serendipitous reasons, I happened upon the unlocked front door of said "dog" establishment and before Nostradamus could explain the idiosyncrasies of the Mayan calendar to Edgar Cayce, Mr. Hot Doug himself was staring kindly back at me from the other side of his sacred threshold of mystical "treats." Of course I was entirely naive to the ritual that I was about to undertake. A char-grilled and deep-fried baptism hadn't been on my conscious agenda for that day. Thank Something that sometimes life takes matters into its own hands. I failed to sense the seductive aura of the unassuming man, who showed no overt signs of being a naturally born cult leader. I must have ordered, but the next thing I remember was his polite jolt to my brainpan: "Have a seat and we'll bring your lunch out to ya. Oh, and help yourself to a soft drink." I don't know if I paid for one or not. But, being a lifelong cola junkie, I zombied my way over to the "help yourself/holy logo machine" and poured myself a refreshingly cold one. I was feeling something subtle closing in on me. What could it mean? Had I somehow spiritually stumbled upon my appropriate place in the cosmic scheme of things? Probably not. My awaiting seat was found on the step-up stage, right in front of the picture window. I remember daydreaming out that porthole for a floating moment, still believing it was the same old reliable world out there. Whether it was or not still remains to be seen.

It's always such a comfort when you sit at a table on your first visit to a restaurant/cult and the table is clean. As I perused the *Sun-Times* for its reliable version of pre/post intellectualism, my lunch arrived as promised. It's true, I had a few conscious and unconscious expectations for my dog and fries. I've driven the dimly lit back alleys of this midwestern hot dog belt. I know a frozen fry when I see one. I know the disappointing texture of a "filler" dog when I taste one. Instead, upon first bite, I sensed the higher callings of my comfort pangs deepen. This lunch was promising to be several notches above my highest standards and I was in the appropriate mood to savor it.

But...let me say that a little louder...BUT(!), nothing could prepare me for the awaiting surprise of the next moment. Rest assured, I do not have access to the literary talents needed to accurately describe just how unlikely that next moment, at that particular time, was for me.

As mentioned, I was either wolfing or scarfing and minding my own business, totally unaware of the seductive forces of brainwashing that were diligently working on my subconscious tendencies. I do remember noticing the punk rock tunes that were tweaked at a nice

volume through the modest house system. The edgy cadence added to the overall ambiance and it all was going rather nicely with my Hot Doug-dog, ice cold drink, and outrageous fries. Any subliminal messages that were most likely massaging my inner ears were flying far afield of my archaic radar screen. Even more interesting was the occasional Madonna, Tom Jones, or any number of mystery alternative bands that I'm probably too old or not "street" enough to recognize. And we're not even to the "Next Moment" yet!

Well look out wienies, because here it comes like an 18-wheeler full of carnival corn dogs, rumbling down the highway at full throttle with no brakes, carnies, candy apples, or cotton candy in sight. All of a sudden, in super slo-mo, I hear my unconscious say to my conscious, "DiD yOu hEaR thAt ThUndEriNg DrUm iNtRo"!!??? DUUUde! Dude's playing tHaT '80s SonG fRom yOuR X bAnd!!! And I'm all... WHAT!!!? So I double-check and this time I'm looking right at the speakers to be certain...and YEP...there "IT" is...in 4/4 time...the relentless backbeat filtered through a touch of electronica, the funk-slappy bass, the wash of guitar orchestration and synth rhythm, and of course,

the desperate and somewhat superficially haunting vocals…

"IT'S A CLEAR * * CUT * * CASE * * * RO-MANTICIDE * * * HOMICIDE * * * * OOOOHHHYYYEEAAHHH"

"Boom***Kack***Boom***Kack*** Boom***Kack***Boom***Ka-chu-cha Boom***Kack***etc."

This style of raging coincidence just doesn't happen to me. I imagine that the way I was smiling ear-to-ear was a bit unsettling as I strolled up to Hot Doug and said . . . "Kind Sir, why are you playing THAT song?" Turns out, it was simply the next tune in rotation on a compilation disk of "one hit wonder" bands from the '80s entitled "Living in Oblivion." While it's not what I would imagine oblivion feeling like, I do believe it's a point well taken.

After listening politely to my explanation, Hot Doug said calmly, "That's cool, how about you sign these liner notes?" Now this was a good 15 years after the original damage had occurred and I was appropriately embarrassed by the suggestion of signing anything. Any intended flattery was undeserved but I got over it, did the deed, and strangely, felt a little bit better for it. How could I foresee the far-reaching implications? While I thought nothing of it, with the scribble of my "John Hancock" it was all Wham, Bam, Now Wasn't That The Plan, All Signed, Sealed, Delivered, and just like that…easily seduced by my own past…I'm officially…in a cult. During my next Hot Doug's visit, my new situation began to slowly occur to me. The only thing left to do was recruit innocent bystanders. If I could find any!

FLAVOUR, FLAVOUR, FLAVOUR

Great food is a celebration of simplicity. It's doesn't need to be fancy and posh. It doesn't have to be ridiculously expensive and served by a regiment of waiters in white. I mean, give me great fish and chips over fussy tasting menus any day of the week. Now, I've been a fan of hot dogs ever since I was a mischievous child growing up Britain. But one sunny day in the spring of 2008 I walked into Doug's joint. I was smitten. The memory remains deliciously vivid because I ate what was without question the finest hot dog of my life. Then I had another. Flavour, flavour, flavour. There are many moments in chilly London when I yearn for a day in Chicago and I dream of a dog done Doug's way.

— MARCO PIERRE WHITE

Celebrity Sightings

While we use the term "celebrity" very loosely at Hot Doug's, we have had our share of real celebrities dine here. It's generally our policy to not broadcast who has been in, as I like to think of Hot Doug's as a safe haven where we don't sausage-narc, my editor pleaded with me and assured me it would be OK to write about it after the fact. I'm still a little dubious, but here goes.

We've certainly had many famous chefs visit, including Anthony Bourdain, Mario Batali (who waited a really long time with his son on a crazy Friday morning), Marco Pierre White, Lydia Bastianich, Grant Achatz, Homaro Cantu, Duff "Ace of Cakes" Goldman (who wore a Hot Doug's t-shirt on an episode of the Food Network's *The Best Thing I Ever Ate*), Graham Elliot Bowles, Paul Kahan, Aarón Sanchez, and many others who I am really going to regret not mentioning, especially when I want to clout a table at their restaurants on a busy Saturday night.

We've also had the pleasure of serving Rahm Emanuel once at the old store when he was running for Congress, and also on his birthday in 2011 when he was running for mayor of Chicago. Actresses Julia Stiles and Anna Kendrick (who did in fact eat her own sausage and then tweeted about it), as well as actors Aziz Ansari, John C. Reilly, John Heard, George Wendt, Fred Armisen, and Nick Offerman have all come in.

Producer Steve Albini, who owns the Electrical Audio studio

> Before shooting the independent film 'Drinking Buddies' at Revolution Brewing's Kedzie Brewery Thursday, Oscar-nominated actress Anna Kendrick ate lunch at Hot Doug's in the Avondale neighborhood. Specifically, the 26-year-old 'Up in the Air' and 'Twilight' star ordered—what else?—The Anna Kendrick.
>
> 'Just had a hot dog called the "Anna Kendrick" at Hot Doug's in Chicago,' Kendrick tweeted about the spicy sausage (which has been named after various attractive celebrities over the years because, as the website says, it's 'Mighty hot!'). 'My mouth is still burning. Awesome awesome awesome!!'

CHICAGO TRIBUNE, JULY 30, 2012
(BY LUIS GOMEZ)

The Anna Kendrick
(formerly the Keira Knightley, the Jennifer Garner and the Britney Spears)
Fire Dog: Mighty hot!
$3.00

yay!

HAPPY AND QUIRKY

Hot Doug's makes me happy! Doug's twist on an American classic is quirky, creative, and inspiring. — **MINDY SEGAL**

MINDY IS THE INCREDIBLY TALENTED CHEF/OWNER OF HOT CHOCOLATE IN CHICAGO. I ALSO HAVE A LITTLE CRUSH ON HER. DON'T TELL HER. I'D LIKE TO KEEP IT A SECRET CRUSH.

Aziz and Doug

AZIZ ANSARI SIGHTING

In 2007 I saw comedian Aziz Ansari perform stand-up at the Lakeshore Theater. About halfway through his set he started talking about all the great food we had in Chicago and went on for maybe 10 minutes about Hot Doug's and its unparalleled deliciousness.

In 2012 I had tickets to see Aziz preform on my birthday, and I went to Hot Doug's for lunch. I was reflecting back on those great Hot Doug's jokes of his and sure enough, there was Aziz, waiting behind me in line to get his encased meat on. **—BOB AGRA**

ACTUALLY AZIZ ANSARI

Hot Doug's is one of my favorite places to eat anywhere. Doug and his food are a class act. I can't write anything else because it will bring up delicious memories that will make me very angry I am not in position to shove delicious Hot Doug's food into my face. See ya soon, Doug. **—AZIZ ANSARI**

EVERYONE WAITS IN LINE

I've become friends with a few fancy chefs over the 25 or so years that I've been a professional cook. The routine is always pretty similar when they come to Chicago. You would probably assume that they all want to head straight to Chicago's gastronomic temples. Not really. Those places require a huge investment of time, and can be an exercise in ego. Hot Doug's is exactly the opposite. The finest encased meats in the land, and a huge dose of hot dog humor. Can Mario Batali or Tom Collichio jump the line? Nope. They are mere mortals at Hot Doug's and have to pay cash like the rest of us. Look for Hot Doug's to receive three Michelin stars in 2014.

— PAUL KAHAN

I, LIKE PAUL, AM A HEIGHT-CHAL-LENGED JEWISH CHEF. WHEN IT COMES TO CULINARY TALENT, THAT'S WHERE THE SIMILAR-ITY ENDS. PAUL'S THE MAN AND ALSO PROVIDES MANY TASTY SAUSAGES FOR HOT DOUG'S.

MARIO BATALI

110 WAVERLY PLACE, NEW YORK CITY, 10003

Dear Hot,

Thanks for the delicious lunch. Your encased meats are an inspiration for weenies like me everyday. We love the HD standard of excellence and are huge fans forever.

Mario and Benno Batali

nearby, has been a longtime and frequent customer, and I've had the pleasure to serve sausages to many of the bands and musicians who've recorded there. Only one time did I ask about a particular band (I like to think it's on the same level as doctor-patient confidentiality). I had read in the newspaper that Iggy Pop and the Stooges were recording at EA. So when the fax order came in, I asked the intern who picked it up if any of the sausages were for Iggy. He said absolutely and pointed out which ones. It's the only EA fax I've saved. And I'm not going to name the intern, as I don't want Steve to can his ass.

We've also had a few musicians perform at the restaurant, including Owen and the Ides of March. Artist extraordinaire Tony Fitzpatrick had a book signing here a few years ago. And ex-Cub Dave Kingman signed his menu board.

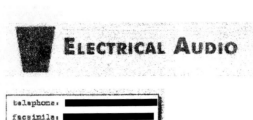

ELECTRICAL AUDIO

telephone:
facsimile:
email:

To: Hot Doug's	From: EA
Fax: 773-279-9553	Pages:
Tel: 773-279-9550	Date:
Re:	Cc:

Qty:	Dogs:	Extras:
1	Veggie Dog	w/ Sport Peppers & Relish.
3	Blue Cheese Pork Sausage	1 w/ NO ALMONDS
2	Corn Dog	
1	JOE AMALFITANO	
1	BALON SAUSAGE	
1	WILD MUSH. + TOM CHICKEN	
1	THE DOG PLAIN!	NO TOPPINGS or CONDIMENTS
1	SMALL CHZ. FRIES	
1	ATOMIC BOMB	
1	CAJUN CHORIZO	
1	DON RICKLES	
1	Small FRIES	

Iggy Pop ✱ ✱

Thank you!

A FEW THINGS ABOUT HOT DOUG'S BY STEVE ALBINI

I admire Doug Sohn and Hot Doug's in enough ways that it is worthwhile to itemize them. I'll start with the smallest one.

He doesn't serve hot dogs with ketchup. Oh, you can get ketchup from the counter and put it on your hot dog if you want, and nobody will bat an eye, but you aren't ever going to get one handed to you that way. It's a small thing but it informs us about a larger thing, a thing that runs like a sinew through the whole of the Hot Doug's enterprise. Doug knows what makes for a good eating experience, and if you just let it happen to you, you'll get one. If you want to fuck it up that's your business, nobody will stop you, but if you just wait in line and order, you'll get something Doug knows firsthand will be satisfying. And Doug knows that hot dogs don't need ketchup.

Doug is there at the counter every day. No matter how often you go there, no matter how much food you order, the guy handing you your food, making change and wishing you well, that's Doug. When Doug goes home, the lights go off. When Doug takes a vacation, the shop is closed. From the first person there for an eye-opener, trying to beat the lunch rush, to the last straggler picking something up for the ride home, every single customer gets to interact directly with Doug. Delegation is one of the many petty uglinesses of contemporary life. If you go to any of the ubiquitous namesake restaurants opened by the nouveaux-chics chefs-célè-bres, odds are that Dude le Chef is somewhere else, maybe on another continent, doing something other than making sure the enterprise with his name on it is upholding his reputation. There's a good chance he hasn't even tasted the food on his namesake menu. Doug's is not run by proxy, it's run by Doug.

Doug comes from Chicago. I don't just mean he lives here, but he grew his teeth, hair, and bones here. I hope he lasts long enough to lose them here. Living in Chicago you see the magnificence of everyday effort all around you. Guys get together and make a punk band or a softball team or labor union or a book club or poker game that survives decades. People don't bitch about the things they lack in their lives, they spit on their hands, lean into the thing shoulder-to-shoulder, and put it up themselves. When the original Hot Doug's burned down, everybody who had come to love it swore curses to all known gods and dreaded each coming daylight. There was a specter of emptiness before us. But because Doug is from Chicago, because he is a punk, he didn't run off crying and abandon this awesome thing. He built another one. Fuck you fire, fuck you fate, you have no idea with whom you are trifling.

Doug built one. One, that's important. He didn't build two, three, or 30 Hot Doug's restaurants, he built one. The one where he goes every day to make food for people, where he gets to hand you your food and say hello, where people line up around the block cheerfully in all weather and never, ever have a bad meal. One. I don't know if it's in a book, but one of the definitions of art ought to be "to do one thing perfectly." Ichiro, Muhammad Ali, Mark Rothko, the Ramones, Studs Terkel, Doug Sohn. All of them do one thing—one seemingly simple thing—and do it so perfectly it transcends its utility and becomes art. If there were two (or 30), then some small part of Doug wouldn't be in the other one (or 29). It wouldn't be perfect.

At last we come to the matter of the food. Fuck me it is delicious. For a couple of bucks you can have the best hot dog on earth. For a couple more, you can have the flavors of fine dining, a perfectly balanced array of tastes and textures served to you by the guy who dreamed it up. Every single thing on Doug's menu is worth your attention. I wish there were a bigger word than "delicious," but fuck me it's all delicious. People who like food make little games of it, like every one of us has his last meal on death row picked out. For the longest time I have maintained that my mother's capelletti in brodo would be mine, but every time I have Doug's duck sausage, a durable part of his special menu, resplendent with its little rondelles of foie gras and fragrant with sweet sauternes, I shiver and beg my mother's forgiveness, because while under its sway I can imagine no better thing to savor as a last taste of earth.

In prison, let us remember. This happens in prison. I'd be in a prison eating a sausage, about to be executed, and happy as a goddamn clam.

World over, Chicago is known as the place where Doug goes to work every day to make hot dogs for people. It isn't a stretch to say I admire and aspire to emulate Doug in my own business. What he does is so good for the food scene and so good for regular people that he makes me want to live up to the reputation he's built for Chicago. I should be so lucky.

Steve Albini is a musician, recording engineer, and studio owner lucky enough to live and work about 400 yards from Hot Doug's.

Owen covers "Summertime Rolls" by Jane's Addiction at Hot Doug's

BY JOSH MODELL / A.V. CLUB JULY 12, 2011

Fate landed Doug Sohn (proprietor of the world's greatest encased meat emporium, Hot Doug's), Mike Kinsella (of Cap'n Jazz, Joan Of Arc, and sole proprietor of the band Owen), and me at the same dinner table a couple of months ago. (The occasion: The Graham Elliot third anniversary dinner. Yum.) Undercover: Summer Break was just an idea at that point, but we immediately hatched a plan to shoot a song at the restaurant (which Anthony Bourdain proclaimed one of "13 places to eat before you die"). We offered to come in after hours, since Hot Doug's is pretty much always packed, but the ever-affable Sohn thought it would be more fun if we filmed while the restaurant was bustling—and he treated us to delicious sausages. The background noise adds some cool layers to Kinsella's sweet, acoustic version of Jane's Addiction's "Summertime Rolls."

RAHM'S BIRTHDAY LUNCH BY JEREMIE MOLL

Entering the line, my coworker and I noticed a well-groomed, suited-up young man in front of us. He stood out because he was alone and constantly checking his Blackberry, though no messages had arrived. He stood out because he appeared a bit nervous as the line continued its march toward the counter. He stood out because he scanned the streets nervously as he entered the front door. But mostly, he stood out because he was actively trying not to stand out.

Once inside, he asked us for recommendations while continuing to nervously fiddle with his Blackberry. Though we provided several suggestions, he heard none. Finally, a look of relief washed over him after which he apologized and once again asked about the menu. It was then that the door behind us opened and a group of five joined him in line. As they passed by us individually, one stood out. I couldn't quite place why at first, but after they had passed I realized that the gentleman was Rahm Emanuel, the lead candidate for the next mayor of Chicago, if only he would make it onto the ballot.

Being a Hot Doug's regular, you get used to seeing celebrities walk through the door to get their sausage fix, with videographers filming their every move. Politicians frequently make campaign stops to glad-hand among the "common folk." Rarely do these types attempt to play it low key—showing up simply to enjoy one of the many distinctive creations on the menu that day. That's what made Rahm's arrival so unique. Walking past us he did not offer his hand for a shake, not because he was rude, but because we did not first offer ours. There were no

cameramen or reporters following behind. He was not there for political reasons, he was there because it was his birthday and that's where he wanted to eat lunch.

Rahm analyzed the many offerings on the menu while the young man—who I now realize was a staffer—asked us if we'd like to have our lunch at Rahm's table. We debated. On the one hand, we really didn't want to sit through a political campaign at lunch; on the other, it would be an interesting story (perhaps one you'd even be asked to write a few paragraphs about in a future book).

So down we sat, just the two of us with Rahm. I noticed his order: The Dog and one of the day's special sausages. A solid order; one that I recommend whenever a new patron asks me what to get. But he never asked, this was his kind of place, he belonged. We talked about schools, casinos, video games, and pinball. We talked about the Cubs and real estate. I told him I was renting a house in the neighborhood; he wished he had rented to me instead of the tenant trying to help keep him off the ballot. He spoke of his visits to Hot Doug's before he was well known, and how this was the place he most wanted to be on his birthday. It was like we were three old acquaintances, catching up on what had gone on in each other's lives over the past few years. For the lunch hour, he was a regular guy, eating at a place for regular guys. Not a single camera. Not a single news mention. Not a single attempt at gaining a vote. Just a single peaceful lunch with this single story documenting it years after.

LIDIA BASTIANICH VISITS

This must have been five or six years ago, in the wintertime. I saw a limo idling in front of the Sausage Superstore for about a half-hour. When Karen (my wife) and I left, we did so sort of quickly, and once outside I turned to her and said, "Wasn't that Lidia Bastianich?" She said maybe and I sort of brushed it off.

Later that day I sent an email to Doug to confirm if Lidia did indeed visit the Sausage Superstore. His reply was, yes it was Lidia. What did he say to her? "Giada, I love your show!"

—LEE BERENBAUM

PATTON OSWALT VISITS HOT DOUG'S

On Christmas Eve 2008, I rushed out of work to get my Hot Doug's fix before he took his winter hiatus. Everything was perfect that day. Not too cold, no long wait, that voice sounds extremely familiar... I turned my head and Patton Oswalt was sitting right there. His wife spotted my eyes widening and my sudden feverish texting as I reported to all my friends that I was mere feet away from one of our favorite comedians. She obviously got a kick out of me being starstruck.

I didn't bother Patton while he was eating. I'm not that guy. But when he was getting up to leave, I didn't pass up the chance to get my picture with him. He was the nicest guy and he eats at an awesome restaurant. —DAVID C. WILLIAMS

David Williams and Patton Oswalt at Hot Doug's.

During my winter vacation, maybe 2008 or 2009, sometime during the week, I found myself in front of a group of people that included Patton Oswalt. He and his friends had gotten out of a cab just as I was parking, and they were right behind me. I went up to him in front of the store and said, "I know who you are." He let me take a picture of him with my phone. When he was inside a few people noticed him, including Doug, but it was very low key. I thought it was very cool, and my boys were excited about it when I told them after I had returned home with the dogs from Doug's.

—**LEAH PRALE UHLER**

Local Celebrity

One of my favorite things about living in a large city like Chicago is the relative ease of remaining anonymous. Well, it used to be one of my favorite things. I do get recognized. It remains an odd feeling, but one I've come to enjoy. Now, I'm not saying I'm the Lindsay Lohan of Avondale (at least not when it comes to being recognized...there may be other valid comparisons, but I don't like to talk about that. I'm sure you understand), but it is an incredibly great feeling to meet someone in public and have them tell you how much they enjoy your restaurant. I'm not going to lie— it's totally cool. Still a little strange, though.

Getting recognized outside of Chicago is particularly odd, and still, I admit it, it's pretty neat. Whether it's been at the airport in San Jose, Costa Rica, or a breakfast place in San Francisco, it's a great feeling. Here are a few of my favorites:

Chez Panisse BERKELEY, CA
Casamento's NEW ORLEANS
Tony Luke's PHILADELPHIA
Spotted Pig NEW YORK
Mama's on Washington Square SAN FRANCISCO

Media Coverage

I'm going to confess: I love getting mentioned in reviews of other restaurants, especially those that feature sausage. Having said that, I still enjoy being featured on TV shows (even though, and you may not believe me, I do turn down a number of requests) and in magazine articles. Small segments on the Food Network (*Heat Seekers, America's Best*) and other TV networks (Planet Green's *Future Food*, History Channel's *Meat America*) have been really fun to film and watch. Brief mentions in magazine and newspaper articles about dining in Chicago are still cool to read. And I really like helping out student filmmakers with their projects (we get asked to do that a lot). The only thing I stipulate is that if the project gets less than an A, he or she is no longer allowed to dine at Hot Doug's. It's a tough love thing.

Funny Stuff

Over the years, I have collected a number of, what I think, are pretty funny articles, letters, emails and the like related to Hot Doug's. I've basically just tossed them in a box marked, go figure, "funny." Writing this book seemed like a fine time to go through the box and share a few of the items.

1. FROM THE *REDEYE* NEWSPAPER, JANUARY 8, 2011

A reader's response to the question, what would be the first thing you buy if you woke up $355 million richer from winning the lottery: "I'd buy Hot Doug's so I'd never have to wait in line."

Just in case you were wondering, I would happily sell you Hot Doug's for $355 million.

2. FROM AN EMAIL IN 2009 CONCERNING OUR SELLING OF FOIE GRAS

"Lucifer has a special place for the likes of you downstairs, its [sic] hot, so It might be hard on your cold heart."

Downstairs?

3. FROM A SUBSCRIPTION ADVERTISEMENT FOR *GRANTA* MAGAZINE

"Granta's latest issue is the hottest thing [in Chicago] since —well—since Hot Doug's started selling duck fat fries."

You'd think a gift subscription would be the least they could do. And not to *Granta* either. Maybe *Hustler* or something.

4. FROM GRUB STREET CHICAGO

June 6, 2010: Doug Sohn Consults On a New Beer and Sausage Bar in Wicker Park

June 24, 2010: Doug Sohn Will Not Consult On a New Beer and Sausage Bar in Wicker Park

5. FROM THE CHICAGO TRIBUNE WEBSITE FRONT PAGE, JULY 23, 2011

Headline: "Hot Doug's temporarily closed due to flooding"

Headline below that: "Amy Winehouse found dead"

6. FROM A HANDWRITTEN NOTE WRITTEN ON A SEARS NEWSPAPER AD AND SHOVED IN THE FRONT DOOR

"why aren't you open till later expect some sodomizing tomorrow you jerks"

They did leave a phone number. I have yet to call.

Favorite Magazine Article Mentions

IN NO PARTICULAR ORDER

1 GOLF DIGEST, SEPTEMBER 1999

I used to play golf, but I had to quit. That hole with the windmill drove me crazy. It's possible I've told this joke at least 300 times at Hot Doug's.

2 MEN'S HEALTH, JUNE 2009

Anthony Bourdain's 13 Places To Eat Before You Die. I love the fact that we're listed in Men's Health. I think it's in the issue that has the article about building up your abs.

3 PUNK PLANET, JULY/AUGUST 2002

My friend Thor Malek used to lament "remember when we were punk?" I got to tell him "one of us still is."

4 CHICAGO MEDICINE, SPRING 2006

"Dr. Herb Sohn Relishes Son's Wienie Success." Sure, they'll print that, but they edited out my line "Yes, we're both in the wiener business." It probably helps to know that my dad is a urologist. See, now it's funny.

5 TODAY'S MACHINING WORLD, FEBRUARY 2008

The magazine for the Precision Parts Industry. I thought that was "Maxim."

6 MOJO, NOVEMBER 2005

The Steve Diggle Sausage Hits Chicago. Plus, the Ramones are on the cover!!

7 DER FEINSCHMECKER, JANUARY 2008

Even they say ketchup ist tabu.

8 SALON.COM, MAY 2007

In an interview with Marco Pierre White, he says "at 4 o'clock he closes the door and he goes home to his family." By "his family," I'm assuming he means "his scotch."

9 URB, MARCH/APRIL 2008

Another Top 100 list, this time it's the 14th Annual Next 100. I'm listed with Ssion, Vince P, and Sankofa. It's possible I don't know what any of that means.

10 B, SPRING 2008

Celebrating Style, Luxury and the Buick Experience. I guess they don't know I drive a 1996 Toyota Corolla. It does have both AM and FM radio, though.

11 PLAYBOY, SEPTEMBER 2011

Porn! Finally!

CHAPTER 6

It's All About the Sausage

The Classic Chicago Hot Dog

The impetus to open Hot Doug's was the Chicago hot dog. It's still the most important menu item and, truth be told, my favorite menu item. It's a great sandwich. A million articles and books have been written about the Chicago-style hot dog, describing its origins, history, and ingredients. I'm not going to expound on that—well, not a lot anyway. ¶ For the uninitiated, the classic Chicago dog consists of an all-beef, natural-casing wiener served in a steamed poppy seed hot dog bun and topped with: **yellow mustard** • **chopped onions** • **sweet neon green relish** (a Chicago thing, don't ask) • **tomatoes** • **dill pickle** • **celery salt** • **sport peppers** (optional). The result: a sandwich chock-full of flavor, texture, and satisfaction. ¶ At Hot Doug's, if you ask for everything on your hot dog (the preferred

YOU'RE NOT SUPPOSED TO PUT KETCHUP ON A HOT DOG
and other food rules you can disregard

In keeping with famous Chicago hot dog lore, ketchup is not included in "everything" at Hot Doug's. When a customer asks for everything and adds "no ketchup," I assure them that ketchup is not part of everything; tsuris like that I don't need.

Having said that, if you want ketchup, we will add it. I know this is a form of blasphemy in Chicago, but I am a firm believer in the mantra that there are no food rules. Eat what you like.

I did turn a little nauseous when I once watched three adults squeeze a whole lot of ketchup on their foie gras sausages (I'm not kidding). That was disappointing. And, as we all know, putting mayonnaise on a corned beef sandwich should seriously be avoided.

suggestion), you will get all of the above except for the sport peppers (you have to ask for those), simply because it's been my experience that the majority of customers don't want them, so why waste them? Also, we substitute caramelized onions for the raw chopped onions when you ask for everything (though we do have raw chopped onions and are happy to make the substitution). Why? Because I think they taste a bit better and, since we caramelize them in butter, it adds another taste and texture to the hot dog.

We sometimes get a bit of grief for that—it's therefore not a true Chicago-style hot dog—but I feel that one of the great things about the Chicago dog is that there are so many ingredients available. You should feel encouraged to mix and match. Some people simply don't like tomatoes or onions or relish or whatever, so of course they're not going to like want the stuff on a hot dog. It's like wine pairing: If you don't like heavy red wine, you're not going to like it more alongside a steak. There are no food rules.

Process of Designing Sausages

I'm often asked how I come up with the different sausages and toppings for the specials list. My smartass response is: "I smoked a lot of dope in college. I could have been a lawyer." I'm not really sure that has anything to do with the sausage-designing process, but it's still kind of true. Unless it's my dad reading this and then I have no idea how this got in here.

The process is, I like to think, the same one any chef goes through when creating a menu. Ideas come from various

influences; these can include prior cooking experience (both professional and home cooking); dining out and seeing what other chefs are doing; reading cookbooks and food magazines; going to markets; walking the aisles of the grocery store, farmer's market, or specialty food store; and traveling to see what other people in the world are doing.

The Idea

I find influences and ideas for new sausages in flavor and texture combinations more than in specific dishes featuring sausage. When I go out to eat, I take note of what chefs are doing with lamb, chicken, or pork, what sauces are popular or work well, and what garnishes they are using.

A BRIEF HISTORY OF THE HOT DOG
Source: The National Hot Dog & Sausage Council

9th Century BC: Homer mentions sausage in the *Odyssey*. Apparently in between fighting monsters and marrying sorceresses, the ancient Greeks found time for what's truly important: encased meats.

1487: The frankfurter is invented in Frankfurt-am-Main, Germany. Or, at some different time, the wiener is invented in Vienna (*Wien* is Vienna in German). Both cities claim to be the originator of the modern hot dog. They should have a dog-off—I bet I could find a few judges.

1600s: Johann Georghehner, a butcher from Coburg, Germany, invents the dachshund, or little dog. He later tries to market his product in Frankfurt. Whether Johann invented the modern hot dog, or someone else did a century earlier (or someone entirely different in Vienna), is hotly contested. (See what I did there?)

1871: Cherles Feltman opens the first Coney Island hot dog stand and the NYC tradition is born.

1893: The Columbian Exposition is held in Chicago. Many hot dogs are consumed and the city is saddled with its greatest legacy: the Chicago-style hot dog.

This is also the year that hot dogs became standard baseball fare, down in Saint Louis—but we won't hold that against the hot dog (go Cubs).

1900-present: A lot of stuff happens, mostly not involving hot dogs. Because why mess with perfection?

The Production

I work with a number of sausage makers and purveyors, as well as many types of food importers and purveyors (cheese, meat, exotic ingredients, and the like). Our sausages are created in various ways. Sometimes a sausage maker will contact me with sausages they've created or want to create. One of the perks of achieving the type of notoriety that we have is that artisans come to us with their wares. I'm not going to lie: going home with a box full of sausage to sample is not the worst thing in the world.

The more common process is working directly with sausage makers to create my concept. We currently work with over a dozen sausage makers and purveyors. Most are local, but we do work with artisans all over the country and Europe. With FedEx and dry ice you can get pretty much get anything from anywhere.

Ribeye Steak Sausage with Chimichurri, Double Creme Brie Cheese, and Crispy Fried Onions.

Taste Testing

Once I come up with the concept I want to serve, then the tasting begins. If we're creating a new sausage, it means going back and forth with the particular sausage maker and adding or subtracting (usually adding) ingredients to make the sausage tastier and bolder. My personal feeling is that if you list an ingredient in the description of the item, you should absolutely taste that ingredient.

Usually the first tasting of the sausage is really good, but it's often not unique or strongly flavored enough, and the type of flavor that I want isn't present. My favorite example is the Über Garlic Sausage. I went back and forth with the sausage maker three or four times, each time with the directive, "Just double the garlic." He would say, "That's too much," and I'd say, "Let me worry about that, let's see what happens." When eating this sausage, I wanted to taste the garlic first and then the pork, not the other way around.

The Toppings

When the sausage tasting is completed and we've come up with the final product, it's time to determine toppings. I often have the complete concept in my head, so I know right away which toppings are necessary. For instance, the Teuben needed to have Russian dressing and sauerkraut because it is a take on the classic Reuben sandwich. Sometimes, it's just working on a particular sauce and then figuring out the sausage that it would best match up with. It can be a quick process (our sauces are relatively simple; they're most often mayonnaise- or mustard-based with flavors added). Three-quarters of our sausages are topped with cheese, simply because cheese and sausage is a perfect combination. And, as my friend Jim O'Grady once told me, I've yet to find a food that's not better with cheese on it.

PHOTO BY ROYA JADE

Once in a while, trying to come up with more unusual toppings takes longer and requires more tastings to get it right. My favorite example is when I wanted to use chocolate on a sausage. One of our customers is the Vosges chocolate company, located nearby. They produce bacon chocolate—essentially dark chocolate infused with applewood-smoked bacon. After numerous trials, I decided to use a dried-cherry-and-apple-infused pork sausage topped with pear purée and Vosges bacon chocolate. My first reaction when tasting the final product was, "I'm not sure this works, but I can't stop eating it." So we threw it on the menu, and it was pretty much an immediate hit.

ASIDE FROM THE SAUSAGE MAKERS, THE MOST IMPORTANT VENDOR I WORK WITH IS THE CHEESE PURVEYOR. LEARNING ABOUT CHEESE AND GAINING ACCESS TO ALL TYPES OF CHEESE IS ONE OF THE MOST EDUCATIONAL (AND ONE OF THE BEST) ASPECTS OF MY JOB. MY CARDIOLOGIST MAY NOT BE THRILLED ABOUT THIS, BUT I'M PRETTY HAPPY. IT'S BEEN A TOTAL JOY MEETING GREAT CHEESE MAKERS FROM AROUND THE WORLD AND SAMPLING THEIR WARES.

I'd say we've designed almost 100 sausages. We don't always use the same toppings, so there are several variations. We may mix and match between two to 10 topping combinations, depending on the sausage. Some are more equipped to handle different types of toppings. It's been awhile since I've given up on a concept or had a failure. In the early days, we weren't able to sell blood sausage. But we recently tried it again and we sold quite a lot of it. Some of this, I think, has to do with customers trusting us more as well as the recent explosion in consumer knowledge and curiosity when it comes to more unusual fare. It may be time to try tongue sausage again.

The BLT: Bacon Sausage with Avocado Mayonnaise, Lettuce, and Roma Tomatoes.

I'm always in the process of creating new sausages. Some of this is simply because it's my job. Also, I like to have something new for our regular customers to try. It's a great motivator and keeps the complacency at bay. We shoot for simplicity—sausage, sauce, topping. That's our style. And the focus is always to make sure it tastes good.

Designer Dogs

People often ask me what's my favorite special and then follow that up with, "It's probably like choosing your favorite child." While I don't have children, I imagine it's easier to love a sausage. Sausages aren't going to stay out past their curfew or ask me for money or get pregnant.

Spicy Thai Chicken Sausage with Sriracha Mustard, Sesame-Seaweed Salad, and Duck Cracklings.

I'm certainly fond of the foie gras sausage, and not just because of the history—I truly love the taste. But really, nothing goes up on the board unless I like it. So I really like everything I sell. The ones that strike a chord with me are the ones whose creation stems from something personal or interesting.

Ale and Chipotle Buffalo Sausage with Bacon-Garlic Mayonnaise and Smoked Gouda Cheese.

Spicy Beef with Coca-Cola BBQ Sauce and Applewood-Smoked Cheddar Cheese.

The Saucisson Alsacienne: Bacon sausage with crème fraîche, caramelized onions, and stinky French cheese. This concept came to me when I was sitting in a restaurant in Strasbourg, in the Alsace region of France. I was eating the local dish, *tarte flambée*. It's essentially a flatbread covered with crème fraîche, *lardons* (bacon), and caramelized onions. As I ate, it occurred to me that we could combine these flavors into a sausage.

The Teuben: Corned beef sausage with Swiss cheese, sauerkraut, and Russian dressing (the name is a play on "Reuben"). I believe it was Mark Schwartz, a.k.a my friend "Biche," who named it the Teuben.

Shrimp and Pork Sausage: Served with Creole mustard, hominy grits, and goat cheese. It's a really nice play on the shrimp and grits idea.

The Portuguese Linguiça: I tend to lean toward smoked pork, particulary this linguiça, which is smoked with saffron rouille and Iberico cheese.

Atomic Bomb: This is a pork sausage flavored with numerous peppers, including jalapeño, habañero, and poblano. It was created in response to customers wanting something super spicy. I'm not a fan of "hot for hot's sake." I think anything spicy should first and foremost be about the flavor, not just the heat. So, while this sausage is pretty damn spicy, it definitely has a lot of flavor.

THE DITKA AWARD GOES TO...

The classic Chicago-style hot dog is hands down the best hot dog Hot Doug's has to offer for a variety of reasons. First, it's priced at or (more often) below the cost of Chicago styles at other famous dog shops. Second, the dog is always piping hot and the veggies are crisp and cold. This is crucial to a Chicago dog—you don't want to be eating a lukewarm handful of mush! And third, its presentation. Every Chicago dog I've gotten from Hot Doug's has looked like it's come straight out of *Sports Illustrated*'s Swimsuit Issue.

Over the course of one day two summers ago, I visited six different Chicago-area hot dog shops in search of the best dog, the place that would receive The Ditka — an award I bestow only to one Chicago-area restaurant that absolutely nails whatever classic Chicago food for which it claims to be known. Hot Doug's secured The Ditka from me without question for the reasons mentioned above, and will continue to be my #1 most-recommended Chicago-style hot dog destination to all who ask. **—PATRICK O'CONNOR**

We asked customers to tell us what their favorite sausages are. There were a lot of opinions, but these rose to the top:

1. **ATOMIC**
2. **TEUBEN**
3. **RIBEYE**
4. **FOIE GRAS AND DUCK**
5. **ÜBER GARLIC**

SOME HONORABLE MENTIONS:

"Ribeye, but I will never, ever forget the glorious Cheesesteak dog." —BRETT McKENZIE WOOD

"There was one that was garlic-and-blue-cheese-stuffed pork sausage. Made me so happy I cried a little." —ERIN TIPTON

"It is difficult to select one favorite. However, when I journeyed there this past winter I was particularly blown away by the kangaroo sausage. Kangaroo is a rare treat; it is tender and lean with just a touch of gaminess. It paired perfectly with the accompanying Saint-Paulin cheese and roasted garlic-chipotle Dijonnaise. Every bite had a creamy, buttery flavor with a slightly spicy kick." —AMBER MICHELLE

"I'm going for a grilled Chicago. Can't beat a classic." —CHRIS CONRAD

"Antelope, antelope, antelope, and any dog with the Molé a la Carlos." —CHRISTINE SAXMAN

CHILI HITS THE SPOT

I can't actually say I've ever eaten a bad thing on the menu at Hot Doug's. Everything has essentially been five stars. The thoughtfulness and harmony of the flavors, and the gourmet influence is so obvious here. Everything is so well thought out and prepared. I like the rotating menu as well. There are some items that are repeated from time to time and never change (Hot Doug's BLT, Sonoran Dog, Beef Sausage with Coca-Cola BBQ Sauce), and there are some that are repeated with one or two things changed (the Linguiça, Mountain Man, Über Garlic, etc.). There are the regular choices (The Foie Gras Sausage, Chicago Dog, Italian Sausage). And from time to time, also, they bust out a DAMN good bowl of sausage chili topped with cheddar and onions. That is a Hot Doug's special appearance, so grab it when you can.

—ROY LICHTER

THE JOHNNY DEPP

I still consider being selected as a finalist in *Time Out Chicago*'s Make Your Own Hot Doug's Hot Dog contest to be one of the most awesome things that ever happened to me. My hot dog, "The Johnny Depp," didn't ultimately win, despite putting together an interstate league of hot-dog-voting voters, but for years I listed it on my online dating profile. Ironically, I ended up getting engaged to a handsome vegetarian, so it's Joe Strummer all the way, from here on out. — **SARAH BEST**

Portuguese Linguiça changed my life. — **VINCE SALVATI**

My favorite has to be the Linguiça... I dream about it. — **SARAH JACOBSEN**

Tequila, Black Bean, and Lime Chicken Sausage.

It's pretty much my job to know what we serve at the restaurant. Having said that, I have truly no idea which sausage this is. It does look darn tasty though, don't you think?

Pecan-Smoked Jalapeño Pork Sausage with Cheese-Stuffed Hot Peppers.

The Paul Kelly and the (at that time) Sally Vega.

BIRTHDAY DOGS

Above: Allen Hurst celebrating his 40th Birthday at Hot Doug's, January 2011; Below: When the Über Garlic is on the menu...you know I'll be at Hot Doug's! —**SHARON HURST**

ATOMIC DOG

I have always said food isn't delicious unless it makes you horribly sweaty. The photo on the left is a candid of me eating the Atomic Bomb, and the other is the aftereffect of eating the sausage. It is one of my favorite pictures and it's the way I would like to be remembered when I pass on.

—**CHRIS MORAN**

Today's Specials

When we moved to the new place, we started using this great "specials" board that allows us to slide sausages in and out as they are available. For this book I decided to go through my boxes and binders of all of those little cards (well, actually, interns at my publishing company went through them. Thanks, Emmitt R. and Danielle G.) to see how many sausages we've created. Here goes...

Aaucisse de Langue

Ale and Chipotle Buffalo Sausage

Ale and Provolone Chicken Sausage

All-Beef Knockwurst

Antelope Sausage

Apple and Cherry Pork Sausage

Apple and Cinnamon Pork Sausage

Apple and Garlic Lamb Sausage

Apple and Gouda Smoked Chicken Sausage

Apple and Habañero Chicken Sausage

Apple and Maple Smoked Chicken Sausage

Apple and Rosemary Chicken Sausage

Apple Chicken Sausage

Apple Pork Sausage

Apple, Pear, and Port Elk Sausage

Applewurst Smoked Pork Sausage

Apricot and Brandy Chicken Sausage

Artichoke and Kalamata Olive Chicken Sausage

Artichoke and Parmesan Chicken Sausage

Atomic Spicy Ribeye Steak Sausage

Bacon and Jalapeño Smoked Duck Sausage

Bacon and Sharp Cheddar Elk Sausage

Bacon Cheeseburger Pork Sausage

Bacon Sausage

Baked Ham Sausage

Beef and Lamb Gyros Sausage

Beef Landjaeger

Beer and Cheddar Cheese Bison Sausage

Beer and Onion Chicken Sausage

Beer, White Cheddar, and Jalapeño Chicken Sausage

Bell Pepper and Mozzarella Chicken Sausage

Bell Pepper, Mozzarella, and Sun-Dried Tomato Chicken Sausage

Bell Pepper Wild Boar Sausage

Blue Cheese Pork Sausage

Blueberry and Merlot Venison Sausage

Boudin Blanc

Boudin Noir

Brandy-Infused Smoked Portuguese Chorizo

Brandy-Infused Sweet Rabbit Sausage

Brown Ale and Chipotle Buffalo Sausage

Bruschetta, Beer, and Portabella Chicken Sausage

Buffalo and Blue Cheese Pork Sausage

Burgundy and Orange Pork Sausage

Burgundy Wine Smoked Buffalo Sausage

Cajun Chorizo

Calvados-Infused Duck Sausage

Caprese Picante Spicy Italian Sausage

Caribbean Goat Sausage

Catalan Butifarra Pork Sausage

Cayenne and Cheddar Pork Sausage

Chardonnay and Jalapeño Rattlesnake Sausage

Cheddar Cheese and Beer Wild Boar Sausage

Cheddar Cheese and Onion Pork Sausage

Cheese-Stuffed Chicken Chorizo

Cherry Ostrich Sausage

Cherry-Infused Venison Sausage

Chicken and Ham Cordon Bleu Sausage

Chipotle and Cilantro Smoked Chicken Sausage

Chive, Pork and Veal Bockwurst

Cognac and Bacon Pheasant Sausage

Cognac and Cranberry Smoked Chicken Sausage

Cognac and Hazelnut Pheasant Sausage

Cognac-Infused Lamb and Pork Sausage

Corned Beef Sausage

Cranberry and Apple Chicken Sausage

Cranberry and Apple Wild Boar Sausage

Cranberry and Cognac Smoked Chicken Sausage

Cranberry and Maple Duck Sausage

Cranberry and Shiraz Wild Boar Sausage

Cranberry and Walnut Chicken Sausage

Cranberry Pheasant Sausage

Creole Chaurice Pork Sausage

Creole Chorizo

Creole-Style Smoked Bison Sausage

Curry Lamb Sausage

Curry Pork and Veal Sausage

Dark Beer and Blue Cheese Pork Sausage

Duck Confit and Pork Sausage

Fig and Brandy Duck Sausage

Foie Gras and Sauternes Duck Sausage

Fresh Mint and Garlic Lamb Sausage

Garlic and Rosemary Smoked Chicken Sausage

Ginger-Spiked Rabbit Sausage

Goji Berry Pheasant Sausage

Hickory-Smoked Spicy Cajun Pork Sausage

Hot Sauce Chicken Sausage

Hungarian Smoked Pork Sausage

Irish Banger

Jack Daniels and Fennel Pork Sausage

Jalapeño and Cheddar Beef Sausage

Jalapeño and Cheddar Pork Sausage

Jalapeño and Monterey Jack Chicken Sausage

Jalapeño Smoked Chicken Sausage

Jamaican Jerk Pork Sausage

Jumbo Slaw Dog

Kangaroo Sausage

Lamb, Pork, and Spinach Loukaniko

Lemon-Pepper Smoked Turkey-Chicken Sausage

Lutefisk and Pork Sausage

Mandarin Orange and Teriyaki Chicken Sausage

Mango and Jalapeño Chicken Sausage

Mediterranean Lamb Sausage

Merguez Lamb Sausage

Mexican Chorizo

Molé and Chipotle Smoked Chicken Sausage

One-Half Pound Holiday Pork Kielbasa

One-Third Pound Calabrese Pork Sausage

One-Third Pound Uncured Pork Kielbasa

Onion Pork Sausage

Pale Ale and Onion Chicken Sausage

Parsley-Infused Weisswurst

Pear and Port Wine Elk Sausage

Pecan-Smoked Jalapeño Pork and Beef Sausage

Pepper and Onion Pork Sausage

Pepper Jack Cheese-Stuffed Chicken Chorizo

Pepperoni and Spinach Pork Sausage

Peppery Cajun Pork Sausage

Philly Cheesesteak Beef Sausage

Pineapple and Jalapeño Pork Sausage

Pork and Beef Curry Sausage

Pork Belly and Lamb Sausage

Port and Cassis Smoked Venison Sausage

Portabella Mushroom and Swiss Cheese Pork Sausage

Portuguese Chourico

Portuguese Linguiça

Quarter-Pound Jumbo Hot Dog

Quarter-Pound Pork Cheesy Grillwurst

Quarter-Pound Smoked Pork Kielbasa

Quarter-Pound Veal and Pork Bratwurst

Red Bell Pepper Wild Boar Sausage

Red Wine and Demi-Glacé Venison Sausage

Ribeye Steak Sausage

Roasted Artichoke Chicken Sausage

Roasted Garlic, Marsala, and Provolone Smoked Wild Boar Sausage

Roasted Pepper and Provolone Pork Sausage

Roasted Red Pepper and Garlic Chicken Sausage

Roman Luganega

Rosemary and Garlic Smoked Chicken Sausage

Saucisse de Morteau

Saucisse de Toulouse

Saucisson Alsacienne

Savory Ostrich Sausage

Smoked and Spicy Cajun Pork Sausage

Smoked and Spicy Kangaroo Sausage

Smoked Antelope Sausage

Smoked Crayfish and Pork Sausage

Smoked Debreziner

Smoked Ham Sausage

Smoked Pork Cheddarwurst

Smoked Portuguese Pork Chourico

Smoked Rattlesnake Sausage

Smoked Shrimp and Pork Sausage

Smoked Yak Sausage

Sonoran-Style Jalapeño-Cheddar Jumbo Hot Dog

South African Beef and Pork Boerwors

Southwestern Bison Sausage

Southwestern Chipotle Buffalo Sausage

Spicy Beef Hot Link

Spicy Italian Sausage

Spicy Pork Hot Link

Spicy Smoked Alligator Sausage

Spicy Thai Chicken Sausage

Spicy Wild Boar Sausage

Spinach and Feta Chicken Sausage

Spinach and Feta Gyros Sausage

Spinach and Feta-Stuffed Pork Loukaniko

Spinach and Mozzarella Chicken Sausage

Spinach, Mozzarella, and Pepperoni Pork Sausage

Sun-Dried Tomato and Basil Pork Sausage

Sun-Dried Tomato and Basil Smoked Chicken Sausage

Swedish Potato Sausage

Sweet and Savory Rabbit Sausage

Sweet Corn and Bell Pepper Chicken Sausage

Swiss Cheese-Stuffed Corned Beef Sausage

Swiss Cheese-Stuffed Pork and Beef Smoked Knockwurst

Taco and Cheddar Pork Sausage

Tequila, Black Bean and Lime Chicken Sausage

The Atomic Bomb Cheese-Stuffed Pork Susage

The "Badger" Beer and Cheddar Pork Sausage

The Frankenwurst

The Mountain Man Sausage

Three Cheese and Beer Chicken Sausage

Three-Chili Wild Boar Sausage

Tomato-Basil Chicken Sausage

Tongue and Cheese Sausage

Tongue Sausage

Truffle-Infused Chicken Sausage

Turducken Sausage

Tuscan Lamb Sausage

Tuscan Wild Boar Sausage

Über Garlic Beef Sausage

Über Garlic Pork Sausage

Veal and Parsley Weisswurst

Veal Saltimbocca Sausage

Veal, Pork, and Chive Bockwurst

White Wine and Dijon Rabbit Sausage

Wild Mushroom and Cognac Turkey Sausage

Wild Rice and Asiago Smoked Bison Sausage

Wild Rice Chicken Sausage

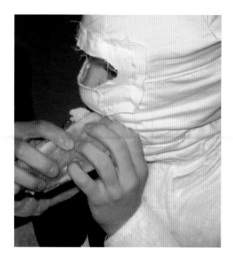

VEGAN CONVERT

I was vegan for nine long, now-inconceivable years. Besides the sack of donuts I finally broke the oath with, the very first real meal I had was at Lula's for Halloween, where Doug sold me a foie gras dog. Here is a photo of me dressed as the band "The Mummies." Incidentally, this was also the first time I ate a Hot Doug's dog, which has started an excellent tradition of consuming fanciful encased meats. I love the varied creations, but honestly, growing up in Chicago with Vienna Beef posters tacked up in every hot dog stand that depict a loaded hot dog barge parked on the lake with a tugboat firing mustard at it, my favorite dog is just The Dog with everything and a mountain of fries. **—MATT CLARK**

Top 10 Fantasy Sausage Suggestions

Editor's note: These suggestions were submitted via Facebook, Twitter, and email. Consequently, the names may not be "real." But we're going with them.

1. **Viking sausage: It'd probably be mead-infused, with lingonberries and goat cheese. —JAMES LEIGH**

2. **The Dirty Whore: Puttanesca-style fish, pepper, and garlic sausage topped with capers, olives, roasted tomatoes, and fried spaghetti. —NILAY GANDHI**

3. **A lobster with pork or something, butter and chives in the sauce, something light for the cheese (Havarti maybe), and bacon bits and crispy fried onions on top. F' yea I'm hungry now. —CHRIS GUO**

4. **The Barnyard: beef, pork, lamb, chicken, and duck. —JOHN RAMEL**

5. **The Pandemonium: panda sausage and bamboo shoots. —VLADIMIR VALCHEV**

6. **I've always wanted to eat a bear. —BRIGETTE VINSON**

7. **Any sausage hand-fed to me by Doug himself is my dream sausage. Would that be named the Creeper? —SHIRLEY HEMPHILL**

8. **Omniscient Sommer: bear and reindeer with lingonberries and chanterelles! —STEFAN SBEPHAN**

9. **The Cookin' More Dog: a frog-leg dog, topped with sliced peaches in a warm brandy sauce, flambéed at the table. —MICHAEL OELRICH**

10. **A unicorn sausage with fried dragon's tongue, double-dipped in the fountain of youth—the most fantastical of all sausages. —BRIAN GERSTEN**

WINE AND PÂTÉ

I remember my first visit to the sausage superstore clearly. The table next to me brought in a $200 bottle of Bordeaux to go with their foie gras hot dog with sauternes. 'Nuff said!—the shwizzle. — **HOMARO CANTU**

FOR THOSE OF YOU WHO DON'T KNOW, HOMARO CANTU IS THE CHEF/OWNER OF MOTO AND ING RESTAURANTS IN CHICAGO. HE'S ALSO DARN FUNNY AND A DAMN FINE CHEF.

PHOTO BY SARAH SIPIL

Another thumb(s) up for Hot Doug's.

—ALLISON BAKER

MOUNTAIN MAN MEMORY

My favorite Hot Doug's memory took place in the summer of 2009. I found myself out of work and living at home, so to pass time otherwise spent looking for jobs on Craigslist and job boards, I'd engage in epic lunch excursions all over the tristate area. On this particular day, I had plans to meet my friend Gwynne for Mexican in Westmont.

Westmont is only about a 30–40 minute drive from Deerfield, and a pretty easy one at that. But with construction, I missed my exit. No problem, I thought to myself. I'll get off at the next one and turn around. Why worry Gwynne with this news? So I loop around so I'm heading the right way again, only now the construction has blocked my exit heading northbound. No reason to panic. I'll call Gwynne and ask for directions. Aware of the construction, Gwynne promptly listed the exits I was to get off at, only by this time, I was too far north so I told her I'd just take the next exit. That was for 90 east.

Having already wasted an hour driving in circles on my Monday, I had no choice but take 90 east to Addison and get in line at Doug's for a Mountain Man. And let me tell you, there's nothing better than spending $8 at Hot Doug's when it's with government-subsidized money as part of your three-hour unemployed lunch break.

I don't know what Gwynne had for lunch.

Epilogue: One week later, I successfully had lunch with Gwynne in Westmont. She drew me a map with directions. The Mexican was fair. **—DANNY WEISS**

DOUG'S KIDNEYS

I worry about Doug's kidneys. He begins his post at the counter at 10:30 each day and stays until 4:00 without a break. He waits on each and every customer, listening to the orders and stories hour after hour. Customer: "I came all the way from Ohio just to eat here." Doug: "I'm sorry."

So, whenever I order, I tell Doug that I will hem and haw and think about what to have while he takes a quick bathroom break. It has to be difficult to be "on duty" for five and a half hours without visiting the sausage emporium facilities. Doug, however, will have none of it. He has a master plan and does not begin drinking any liquid until late in the afternoon. Try as I may, he has never taken me up on my offer.

— **CAROLYNNE SANDERS KENT**

AS MENTIONED ON PAGE 29, MY DAD IS A UROLOGIST. DRAW YOUR OWN CONCLUSION.

A DAUGHTER'S LOVE

By the time you read this, I may be in prison for murdering my mother. Either involuntary manslaughter or premeditated murder—you be the judge.

On a recent Friday, I took my 73-year-old hot dog/pizza loving Michigan residing mother to Hot Doug's. I took her here knowing full well that after her quad bypass a few years ago, the last thing her heart doctor said to her was, "Remember, Jean, the two worst things a heart patient can eat are hot dogs and pizza." So what did I do during her visit? I took her to Palermo's on 95th one night and Hot Doug's 18 hours later.

We waited 80 minutes in line down the block in 80 degree heat. She never complained—in fact, we bonded. And all the while my vegetarian friends were texting me, "Don't do it! Leave now! Don't get the duck fat fries, either. You are killing your mother."

As I am neither Jewish nor Catholic, I do not possess one modicum of guilt. However, as we approached Doug to place our order, I did do one thing he has probably never seen a customer do. As I placed my order, I mouthed the words "duck fat" when ordering the fries, then I pointed at my mom and winked. He got it.

My mom loved her Elvis sans her usual ketchup—a Polish sausage "Smoked and savory—just like the King." Thank god she didn't embarrass me by ordering ketchup on it—I had had THAT talk with her in line, about how it is virtually considered illegal to order ketchup on Chicago encased meat. (I think I read Mayor Daley is planning a tax on that soon, also.) I ordered the Laura Leighton—an Irish Banger with Goose Island Honker's Ale Mustard and Irish Harp Cheddar Cheese. Fantastic!

As of this writing, my mother is still alive and still reminding me that every time she comes for a visit, she wants to go back to Hot Doug's. I can't think of a better compliment. —**DEBORAH ELSTON**

A DAUGHTER'S REWARD

My daughter, Allison Conrad, had just finished her freshman year of high school and was allowed to select a reward for her good grades. She chose duck fat fries! — WENDY GUNDERSON

PHOTOS BY WENDY GUNDERSON

HOLD THE CHEESE

My first visit to Hot Doug's was on a Friday, which meant the fries were done in duck fat. Having never enjoyed the goodness of food prepared in duck fat, I got to the counter and asked Doug for cheese on my fries. His response? A simple head shake with a smile: "No. I won't do that for you. Not today. I can't ruin these fries with cheese. If you WANT, I'll give you some on the side, but I won't put cheese on these fries." My husband (an obsessed and avid patron for years now) tells this story to anyone and everyone going to Chicago, after he mentions Hot Doug's as a MUST for lunch. —ABBY ALWAN

WELL, I GUESS THERE IS ONE FOOD RULE. WE STILL WON'T PUT CHEESE ON THE DUCK FAT FRIES. I'M STUBBORN THAT WAY.

PHOTO JEFFREY ALBERT PAHATI II

Submit Your Haiku
Oh Yes, My Encased Meat Friends
Keep Up the Good Work

—*HOT DOUG*

COULDN'T DECIDE

— **JIMMY RAMIREZ**

Is the wait worth it?
The answer comes when I reach
the jackalope. Yes!
— *FINCH GRACE*

Chicago winter
Do your wurst
The line may be shorter
— *MARK EBLE*

No words are finer
In the English language than:
Encased meat, my friend
— *DAVE SWANSON*

I like my hot dog
Why yes it is rattlesnake
I don't mind the line
— *SEAN SLATTERY*

Fries fried in duck fat
No need to dip in ketchup
Purely good untouched
— *DREW GASCON*

Oh, joyous sausage
Laying, tranquil, in your bun
Amid condiments
— *SUSIE McCORMICK*

A brat in a bun
Soaked in beer nice and juicy
Hello, Paul Kelly
— *JILL YOUNGMANN OLDHAM*

Long, slow-moving lines
Frustrate, unless they lead to
Encased meats, my friend
— *BRIAN COOK*

Anticipation
Scan menu, drool, scent of meats
then Doug yells out, "Nexxxxxxxt!"
— *RYAN REZVANI*

Wind blows on Roscoe
A line of hungry diners
The Steve Swisher, grilled
— *MIKE ANSON*

Rattlesnake, ostrich
Animals encased for me
Doug completes my dream
— *DAVID LOTA*

Thirty dollars gone
It matters not. The deep spend
Makes my tastebuds smile
— *GRANT SMITH*

Beef pork and garlic
Rep'd by Crosby and Allen?
Doug's a hockey puck!
— *JUSTIN ULLMAN*

Eating with Elvis
Encased meat, imported cheese
We all become kings
— *MICHAEL OELRICH*

Your lines are too long
Although we love your meat, Doug
Time robs you of ME
— *MARK IVAN*

No matter the wait,
Encased meats shall be devoured,
Bring on the duck fat fries!
— *ANNE GERACI LOMBAUER*

Editor's note: We asked for haiku submissions over Facebook and were overwhelmed with submissions. Because they were submitted through Facebook, Twitter, and email, we can't vouch for the names of the contributors. We can, however, vouch for the poetry.

HOT DOUG'S MENU IN HAIKU BY TUCKER KEATLEY

....

The Dog

Ole Chicago, MY!
Classic Town Trimmings, 'Nuff said.
Lo, THE MIGHTY DOG!

The Elvis

Ye Poles now REJOICE!
Hunka-Hunka Burnin' Love
Eat, Rock, Like the King.

The Paul Kelly

Bratwurst, beer-soak'd Joy,
fill my belly, cake art'ries,
O' Brat! Fulfillment.

The Sal Tessio

Ruthless Italian
Sausage, strictly delicious.
Dog you can't refuse.

The Anna Kendrick

Too hot for you, Sir.
Spicy, beautiful. O' My!
Beware o Anna.

The Brigitte Bardot

Handled Anna? HA!
French Fire Dog o my nightmares
makes Hell seem freezing.

The Norm Crosby

Cased Germania!
Multimeat heaven, BEHOLD!
Garlic Normdog, Ho!

The Joe Strummer

Veggie fans, be glad!
No meat? Stress not, Ye can eat!
For three bucks: Bodhi.

The Steve Swisher

Cluckerdog two ways
Ye won't Catch cholesterol,
Glory in its gaze!

The Dave Pound

Stay out of the pound
with this fried hound, golden
You'll be beholden!

The Charlie and James Sohn

Kiddies most welcome
devour these bagel-dogs
Quiet, eating tots.

Duck Fat Fries

My quacking friend, Thanks.
You gave your life up for us,
Your death, not in vain.

HOT DIGGITY-DOUG! BY KATIE DAVIS

When we initially heard about the infamous Hot Doug's and that it was in Chicago, we knew the next time we were in the city we would have to make a visit, which happened to fall right after New Years, 2010, when were headed through Chicago on our way back to Dallas. This was when we first learned that they often take off on holidays and, in this case, extended vacations, so they would not be open at all while we were in the city. We were extremely bummed, but said we would just have to make it a priority on our next visit, which happened six months later when we were in the city for a bachelor/bachelorette party. Well, no such luck this time either, because they were closed again for a holiday.

As they say, the 'third time is a charm.' When we came back to Chicago for the wedding, we were lucky enough to pull up and see a line literally out the door and around the corner. I wasn't so happy to see the line, but hey...at least I knew they were open! And, although I did not really want to wait (I'm impatient like that), knowing this may be our only shot, we hopped in line and waited the hour it took us to get to the counter.

We finally made our way in and were able to gander at the menu for a little bit to determine what we should order. In addition to their typical menu items (which are far from typical), they have daily specials that are over the top unique. I knew I wanted simple so I could taste their quality without a lot of other flavors throwing me off, so I went with "The Elvis"—a polish sausage topped with mustard, ketchup, caramelized onions, relish, and pickle. Adam chose to be more adventurous and went with their "Game of the Week," a beer and cheddar bison sausage. He also doubled his pleasure by ordering one of their specialty sausages, the swiss cheese smoked pork knockwurst with bacon-garlic mayonnaise and vintage van Gogh cheese; and we, of course, ordered a large duck fat fries to share.

Deeeeeeee-licious! Needless to say, we were stuffed by the time this meal was over; and I usually don't condone eating past the point of being full, but I didn't let a single one of those duck fat fries go to waste. Those are kind of a once in a lifetime

sorta thing. In all, we were very pleased with our meal, especially considering how long we had to wait to try it...definitely worth it!

Review of Taste: I enjoy hot dogs and sausages, but I would hardly call myself a connoisseur. I know what I like and don't, and these definitely rank at the top of the like list. The polish sausage had a nice snap to it, but was definitely juicy inside. Its flavor was distinct yet tasted familiar as well. I truly enjoyed how all the condiments rounded out the sausage and those duck fat fries...simply delish. Adam also enjoyed his two picks, one more than the other I believe, but surely seemed to enjoy the rich flavors of the meat paired with the unique condiments. Overall: 4½ 'Little Piggies.'

Excerpt adapted from "Hot Diggity-Doug" article on PopCultureCuisine.com, January 14, 2011

HOT DOG UNIVERSITY

I took this picture of Doug and Mike Helminiak. Mike is an independent distributor who supplies Doug with his Vienna Beef products. I am the founder of Hot Dog University and partnered with Vienna Beef in 2009. I knew Herb Sohn, Doug's father, before Doug was born. Herb, a urologist, was a customer at Mal's Pharmacy in Chicago, where I worked part-time as a teen. I hadn't seen Herb since the '60s and ran into him at the Tall Ships, US Cellular Days in Kenosha in the 2003, where I was a vendor. That's when I discovered that his son, Doug, had opened the original Hot Doug's. Like father, like son, both in the weenie business!

I've been selling hot dogs since 1955. Hot Dog University has trained over 700 students since 2006. While most open a cart business, more than 30 percent open hot dogs stands like Doug did. I always take them on a field trip to Hot Doug's to observe what a truly successful business is all about. —**MARK REITMAN**

WE EAT EVERYTHING AT HOT DOUG'S

BY SERIOUS EATS CHICAGO (chicago.seriouseats.com), June 11, 2012

On June 9, 2012, the Serious Eats Chicago crew met up in Avondale to accomplish one of the most glorious eating projects in Chicago history: to eat every single item at Hot Doug's. Why? Without a doubt, this "sausage superstore and encased meat empo-

rium" is the busiest hot dog stand in Chicago and is often mentioned as the best in the nation. While other writers have sought to capture the essence of the experience, we were only interested in the meat. Until now, all of us had only eaten it piecemeal. But we wanted the whole picture, and there was only one way to do that.

We waited in line like everyone else, patiently checking the time before the doors opened at 10:30 a.m., when we all rushed in. We knew that owner Doug Sohn would be there—he's always there—but we didn't expect him to be so focused and ready.

Sure, he knew we were coming (it was the least we could do) but we didn't expect him to have the order already written out and ready to go. All he had to do was hand it to his crew and the feasting would begin.

The actual eating process was a blur. The sausages started coming out of the kitchen so quickly we had a hard time keeping track of them all. Though 10 insatiably hungry eaters came to battle every sausage at Hot Doug's, you better believe that the encased meats won. We tried our hardest, but with over 25 different items, we barely made it out alive.

But let's go over the basics, shall we? Hot Doug's has two menus, a regular menu that, with exception of a few name changes over the years, stays the same. Here you'll find such classic sausages as the bratwurst, Polish, and the natural casing Vienna Beef hot dog. Each can be ordered up exactly as you'd like, though we definitely recommend asking Doug what he prefers. His suggestions are always spot on.

But Hot Doug's is probably most famous for its chalkboard menu of Daily Specials, a collection of composed sausages that pair exotic sausages with some truly surprising toppings. This is where you'll find items like a Spicy Thai Chicken Sausage with Sriracha Mustard, Sesame-Seaweed Salad and Duck Cracklings and an Irish Banger with Guinness Mustard and Carrigaline Farmhouse Cheese. As the label suggests, these offerings change constantly, so even though we ate everything on the menu on our visit, items pop up and disappear regularly. Always check with the website if you want to know for sure. But you can rest assured you'll find the notorious Foie Gras and Sauternes Duck Sausage with Truffle Aioli, Foie Gras Mousse and Fleur de Sel, which earned Sohn the very first fine during Chicago's brief foie gras ban.

When the two menus are combined, you're left with 23 different sausage options. But, wait! There's more!

With so many tempting sausage choices, it's probably best that Sohn keeps it simple with the sides. Besides the tater tots that come with the mini-bagel dogs, fresh-cut french fries are your only choice of a side during the week. The weekend, however, is a different story. On Friday and Saturday you can also order duck fat fries, which, as the name suggests, are cooked in duck fat. We ordered both, along with an order of cheese fries, which use the regular fries.

Doug, as always, was gracious and accommodating throughout this crazy project. We truly couldn't have done this without his help, or the heroic effort from his crew. Honestly, they all couldn't have been nicer about the whole thing. Thanks!

"DOUG, BRING ME ONE OF EVERYTHING... NO SERIOUSLY..."

— ZACHARY POZULP, JANUARY 2012

TO THE BEST OF MY KNOWLEDGE, THE QUOTE "ONE OF EVERYTHING" HAS BEEN ORDERED ON THREE OCCASIONS. "ONE OF EVERYTHING" IS ALSO MY ANSWER TO THE DREADED QUESTION, "WHAT SHOULD I GET?" THUS FAR, NOBODY HAS TAKEN MY ADVICE.

The Foie Gras Affair

A couple of years into the store, we started serving a foie-gras-and-duck-meat sausage. It was topped with brown mustard and caramelized onions (as were virtually all of our specialty sausages in the beginning). I love foie gras, and I also thought it would be funny for a hot dog stand to serve such a high-end and expensive ingredient. Also, did I mention that I love foie gras? I was certainly aware of the negative opinions around how foie gras is made. But at that time, it wasn't a huge controversy or at the forefront of food talk, as it is now.

It all started with California passing a law in 2004 that, beginning in 2012, would prohibit the production and sale of foie gras. Somehow, a Chicago alderman who shall remain nameless, thought this was a great use of city council resources and decided to pursue a similar foie gras ban. This sparked a lot of debate over foie gras and whether it should be government controlled. Lots of restaurants and individuals argued that it was like smoking cigarettes: a personal choice that shouldn't be prohibited. Animal rights groups got involved and lobbied heavily in favor of the ban.

In the end, the city council passed the ordinance in 2006 and Chicago became the first city to officially outlaw the sale of foie gras. That really could have been the end of that story—no one could have predicted the insanity that would ensue.

So the law said restaurants could not serve foie gras in any form. But there was no language about buying it from wholesalers, or about consumers consuming

PHOTO BY ROYA JADE

Foie Gras and Sauternes Duck Sausage with Truffle Aioli, Foie Gras Mousse, and Fleur de Sel.

it. We (by which I mean me), being somewhat of a contrarian, sort of thought, well, whatever, we're going to keep selling it, in part just to see what would happen. After the law passed, there was about a six- or eight-month period before it was enforced. During that window of time we got a warning letter saying we were in violation of this upcoming law. Hot Doug's was the first restaurant in Chicago to receive this letter. I framed it and displayed it on the counter. This was not a political statement; it was purely to be a smartass. We continued to have it on the menu.

A few months after that, we received our second warning letter. At this point, the law had still not gone into effect.

Then the law went into effect. We continued to serve the foie gras sausage.

We got calls and emails, people calling us not-so-kind names. But now I was digging my heels in a bit more. And did I mention that we started calling the foie gras sausage "The Joe Moore?" Yes, we did, my friends (he might be the alderman we are refusing to name).

It turns out, much to my chagrin, that the Chicago health department didn't share our sense of humor. I'm not sucking up here, but I like to point out that the health department didn't want to deal with this. Enforcing the law got dumped in the department's lap. I sympathized; this law was taking away time and energy from the health department's actual job, which is to protect the health of restaurant patrons.

Anyway, they made it known very quickly that they didn't find the situation amusing and that they would be conducting res-

"The city has sent warning letters to nine restaurants believed to have served foie gras but has issued no citations, said Chicago Department of Public Health spokesman Tim Hadac. Letters are sent after a citizen complaint and are followed by a visit after a second complaint... . 'In a world of very limited public health resources, we're being asked to drop some things so we can enforce a law like this,' Hadac said. 'With HIV/AIDS, cancer, West Nile virus and some of the other things we deal with, foie gras is our lowest priority.'"

RED EYE, AN EDITION OF THE *CHICAGO TRIBUNE*, DECEMBER 21, 2006

"When Doug Sohn shuttered up shop last summer after a Roscoe Village blaze wreaked havoc on Hot Doug's, his encased meats emporium, corndog-dependent children and children at heart city-wide were forced to put their char-broiled hunger pains on ice.

But this January, while Chicago was buried under mounds of frost and slush, Sohn fired up his grill at a new location. Saliva glands from Humboldt to Hyde Parks began to thaw, reawakened by the aroma of dogs of every breed (chorizo, bratwurst, ostrich and Polish, among them)."

UR MAGAZINE
FEBRUARY 17- MARCH 16, 2005 ISSUE
(BY JENNIFER WEHUNT)

> In one of those only-in-Chicago moments, a Northwest Side hot dog joint recently became the first eatery to officially run afoul of the city's new foie gras ban.
>
> Doug Sohn, proprietor of Hot Doug's, was ticketed, paid a $250 fine and earned national attention, including an appearance on ABC's 'Nightline.'
>
> With 30 pounds of the banned product sitting in the restaurant's freezer, a Chicago police officer lunching at the popular storefront was overheard asking one of Sohn's employees what would happen to the duck liver delicacy.
>
> Sohn has been contemplating just that.
>
> 'Most likely I'm going to donate it—I have friends in the restaurant business, caterers, who are in the burbs,' he told the *Sun-Times*.
>
> 'I've also thought about getting a cart and standing on the Evanston side of Howard and screaming "Everyone now, get your foie gras here."'

CHICAGO SUN-TIMES, APRIL 18, 2007
(BY LISA DONOVAN)

> In the end, Doug Sohn decided to pony up, not duck. An attorney for Sohn, proprietor of the Northwest Side's 'encased meats emporium' Hot Doug's, appeared Thursday before the Chicago Department of Administrative Hearings and agreed to the $250 fine lodged against the hot dog stand for selling the foie gras-laced sausage.
>
> That makes Sohn the first official violator of the city's seven-month-old ban on the duck liver delicacy.

CHICAGO SUN-TIMES, MARCH 30, 2007
(BY JANET RAUSA FULLER)

City of Chicago
Richard M. Daley, Mayor

Department of Public Health

Terry Mason, M.D., F.A.C.S.
Commissioner

Food Protection Division
2133 West Lexington Street
2nd floor
Chicago, Illinois 60612
(312) 746-8030
(312) 744-2960 (TTY)
http://www.ci.chi.il.us

Hot Doug's
3324 North California Avenue
Chicago, IL 60618

September, 2006

NOTICE OF CO
VIOLATION OF CHICAGO

As of August 23, 2006, the Chicago ban
and 7-39-005) went into effect, which pro

The City has received a complaint that y
Food Establishments – Banned items o
owner you are in violation of the ban if y
sale.

This letter serves to warn you that upon
your establishment an inspection will en
are found during the inspection, a citation

If you have any questions about the Chi
can be found on the City of Chicago's we

Sincerely

Terry Mason, M.D. F.A.C.S.
Commissioner

NEIGHBORHOODS
Alive!
BUILDING CHICAGO TOGETHER

Chicago Department of Public [Health]
Food Protection Divis[ion]
Food Establishment Inspect[ion]
Form - 1410

License #:	Inspection Type	Re-Inspection of Insp. #	Date
1546162	6		

Date of Inspection	Time Started:	Time Completed:	Sanitarian Badge #	Supv. Badg[e #]
4/5/07	12 10	1220	397	321

Business Address
3324 N. California

	Zip Code	Lo[...]
	18	

DBA
Hot Dougs

AKA Hot [...]

Name of Certified Manager On Duty
Douglas Sohn

Certificate # HWS-6208

Illinois law requires that the individual performing your inspection is tested and certified or works [...] Environmental Health Sanitarian.

Violation #	
48	No inspection conducted at t[...]
48	On premises to remove tag from p[...] stored in basement freezer, instruc[...] Code of the city of Chicago 7-39-00[...] Banned items - All food dispensing e[...] cited in section 4-8-010 of the munic[...] hibit the sale of foie gras

7-42-070 REINSPECTION FEE: A $50 re-inspection fee shall be assessed against the Licensee of any e[...] Department of Public Health to address a violation previously identified by the department.

Sanitarian Signature
J. Wall[...]

Signature of Person Report Discussed With

White Copy: Chicago Department of Public Health / Food Protection Division   **Yellow Copy** [...]   **Pink Copy** [...]

Form LG 1410 - Revised: CL-5-06

ADMINISTRATIVE NOTICE OF ORDINANCE VIOLATION
In the City of Chicago Department of Administrative Hearings
City of Chicago, a Municipal Corporation, Petitioner, vs.

Respondent if Chicago Business, use name on license   **Last Name, First Name** **MI**
Hot Dougs

Resp. Address No.	Dir.	Street Name	ST Suffix	Apt./Ste.
3324	W	California	Av	

City   **State** ☒ IL ☐ Other: **ZIP** 60618

Person Served if other than the respondent   **Last Name, First Name** **MI**
Sohn, Douglas

Phone 1-773-799-5[...]   **Acct. No. or DREV No. on business license** 2080098-[...]

Identification ☒ DLN/ID ☐ Other		IL	☐ Other:	**D.O.B. (M/D/Y)** 01.8[...]
S50-0176[...]026				

Height	Weight	Sex	Race	Eyes	Hair	**Service Request Number**
510	160	M	W			120297

Officer, Investigator, Inspector, and/or Complainant on oath states that the Respondent did then and there violate the following section(s) of the Municipal Code of Chicago:

H0003 5433 11

COUNT		COUNT	
	FOOD HANDLING / SANITATION CERTIFICATES 7-38-012		PREVIOUS SERIOUS AND / OR MINOR VIOLATIONS NOT CORRECTED 7-42-090
	CONTROL OF VERMIN AND INSECTS 7-38-020		HEALTH SUMMARY REPORT POSTING 7-42-010(b)
	COMPLIANCE WITH CITY HEALTH REGS 7-38-030		CONDITIONS DETRIMENTAL TO HEALTH / NUISANCE 7-28-060
	FOOD HANDLING / FOOD PROTECTION REQUIREMENTS 7-38-005(a)		**OTHER:** TITLE CHA.SEC. 7-39-001 **RULE**
	APPROVED FOOD SOURCES, WHOLESOMENESS, PROPER TEMPERATURE 7-38-005(b)		Offense (if other): Food establishment
	FOOD HANDLING EMPLOYEES - HYGIENE / CLEANLINESS 7-38-010(a)		Banned item.
	FOOD HANDLING EMPLOYEES - INFECTIONS / DISEASE 7-38-010(b)		

You Must Describe Actions for Each Count below:

Count 1, In That: Found foie gras for sale on premises, as described [...] to remove [...]

Count 2, In That:

Violation Location Nos.	Dir.	Street Name in the City of Chicago, County of Cook	ST Suffix
3324	N	California	Av

Vio. Date: Mo/Day	Year	Time of Violation ☒ AM ☐ PM	Notice Date: Mo/Day if different than Vio. Date	Year of Notice 20
03/16 20		07 1:00		20

Health Version 03-02

Complainant's Name if not issuing officer, investigator, or inspector

Unit	Star / Badge	Signature of issuing officer, investigator, or inspector
	397	X

Administrative Hearing Appearance

IMPORTANT: You must appear for a mandatory hearing on:

Date: Mo/Day	Year	Time	☐ AM ☐ PM
03.29	2007	9:00	

☒ 400 W. Superior   ☐ 2550 W. Addison
☐ 800 N. Kedzie   ☐ 4770 S. Kedzie
☐ 2006 E. 95th St.   **Room No.** 112

FAILURE TO APPEAR may result in the imposition of a fine not to exceed the maximum penalties for each violation as specified in the Municipal Code of Chicago plus costs, restitution, and fees. Failure to comply with the administrative law officer's order may result in the issuance of additional sanctions.

I acknowledge receipt of this notice.
Signature of Respondent or Person Served: X

H

Comments 1-Foie gras

RESPONDENT COPY

[NOTIC]E OF ORDINANCE VIOLATION

[...] THE DIRECTIONS BELOW)

[...]on on the date and time reflected on the [...] entered against you. Fines not to exceed [...] Municipal Code of Chicago for each [...]ay be imposed.

[...] enforced through wage garnishment, [...], and the imposition of liens on real [...]ding but not limited to attorneys' fees [...] to the City.

[...] that necessary witnesses are present

[...] law officer's order may result in the

[...]ations cited in this Notice or the [...]t of Health at (312) 746-8030. [...] hearing process, contact the [...]12) 742-9032.

taurant inspections at very inopportune times for us, like noon on a Friday, one of our busiest days. But we continued to poke the bear.

Friday, February 16, 2007, was the penultimate day we were going to be open before we closed for a two-week vacation. Incidentally, I was traveling to the Alsace region of France, the home of foie gras. So I figured, all right, we're going to be closed for two weeks and it's the end of the work week, we're going to have some fun. I put on the menu three different specials that had foie gras in them: one had foie gras in it, one of the sauces consisted of foie gras, and the third one had a foie gras pâté on top. My feeling was, it's a Friday, we'll put it on there, we'll be fine.

Apparently, someone who I like to think had too much time on their hands was monitoring our website and the specials. I put the list up on our website specials page at 7:00 that morning and when I got to work, shortly before 10:00 a.m., the health department was knocking on my door. They had seen that we had foie gras on our specials board and they started going through everything with a fine-toothed comb. They effectively stopped us from serving the customers who had started to come in.

Even though we hadn't actually served any foie gras that day (we erased it from the specials board), I was not going to point that out to the health department. I had not only my living to worry about, but also the staff who worked there.

DEAR ASSWIPE

During this time period, the overwhelming majority of my customers were either very supportive or didn't have strong feelings one way or another about the issue. But there were a few people, all of whom were not customers, who were less pleased about our stance on foie gras. My personal favorite email began with "Dear Asswipe," and continued to comment about the sexual proclivities of my mother and the manner in which I came into being. A few other letters asked how I'd like to have a tube shoved down my throat and be force-fed. If I was force-fed hot dogs and scotch, I say OK. We were also dissed by a Toronto newspaper, which, nothing personal against Torontonians, but between that and Hedo Turkoglu single-handedly killing my 2009 fantasy basketball team, I may be not so keen on our fine city to the north.

The health department confiscated all the foie gras product we had. They tagged it and we had to store it in the basement freezer for future inspection. We're talking about 100 pounds of sausage and 5 pounds of fresh foie gras. Probably $1,100 in product.

So we took it off the menu that day and Saturday, and then we went on vacation for two weeks. We were ticketed on that Friday for $250. We were the first and I think only restaurant to be fined for selling foie gras. Other places were serving it but not actually "selling" it.

I left for France on that Sunday. One of my favorite anecdotes from this time is that while I was sitting in O'Hare, waiting for my flight, CNN was on the TV and the crawl said: "Hot Doug's fined for serving foie gras in Chicago." Look at that!

I came back, we reopened, and foie gras was not on the menu. It wasn't a political thing—whatever my moral and ethical feelings about it, it just wasn't a big enough issue to make a stink about it. One of my arguments against the anti foie gras coalition is the waste of time and energy on a trivial issue. I was not going to be hypocritical and spend equal time and energy on the other side of the argument. For the next six to eight months, we didn't have it on the menu. I enjoyed being in business, I was happy to have a staff, and it's just a duck.

Completely unbeknownst to me, the law was going to be overturned. I had no idea until the night before when I got a call from a reporter asking for a statement. My response was, "I had no idea." And I was curious about how it happened. I was asked if I felt like I fought the law and I won, and my feeling was more like, no, I ignored the law and only kind of won. We took a bullet, but we offered no resistance.

From that point on, we started selling the foie gras sausage again, and have been selling it ever since.

It was a fascinating period of time, mostly because I got to see how the city government worked. I truly think we were targeted by the pro foie gras forces to

I made this a few years back when Doug was the first violator of the foie gras ban. My girlfriend and I were going to make these t-shirts (to parody the recently popular FREE WINONA ones), but luckily the whole thing was over with so quickly that it wasn't even much of an issue.

—JOHN LOMBARDO

Front page news!
We couldn't be prouder.
And we feel compelled
to back your fight!
You go boy!

Kim   Aly alex Linda
                    Tavounli

show how it wasn't only going to affect high-end restaurants. Laws like this can affect small independent hot dog stands too, which are the cornerstones of Chicago.

The episode also raised important ethical questions about how we get foie gras specifically, and how we get food in this country in general. These are valid and important questions that we should continue to ask.

A month or two later, I asked a friend who works in PR how much would it would have cost to have publicity like what I got for the Foie Gras Affair—all I'd paid was $250 for the fine. "You can't pay for this kind of publicity," was her response. "But if you could... you did very well."

Apparently the pro-foie faction was a big enough pain in the ass about this, because the Chicago city council voted to overturn the ban in 2008—just two years after the law was enacted. I think the reversal was partly because of the fuss people made over personal freedom to ingest whatever they wish, and partly because of outrage that his was how the city council was choosing to spend its time. I would certainly think this city has a lot more pressing issues to deal with than whether or not restaurants can sell duck liver pâté.

It helps that Daley was quoted by numerous news media as saying that the ban was the silliest law ever passed in Chicago. Daley on your side gets you pretty far in this town.

Desmond Green, still outraged by the Foie Gras Affair, shows his retroactive support for Hot Doug in 2012 with his "Free Hot Doug" t-shirt and conspicuous lack of pants.

Mayor Daley calls the ban the 'silliest' law. Restaurants across town serve up the delicacy in defiance. Now the question is whether city officials will actually try to enforce the new law.

EXCERPT FROM "CHICAGO'S WILD FOIE GRAS CHASE" IN THE *CHICAGO TRIBUNE*, AUGUST 23, 2006 (BY JOSH NOEL, BRENDAN MCCARTHY, AND JAMES JANEGA, TRIBUNE STAFF REPORTERS)

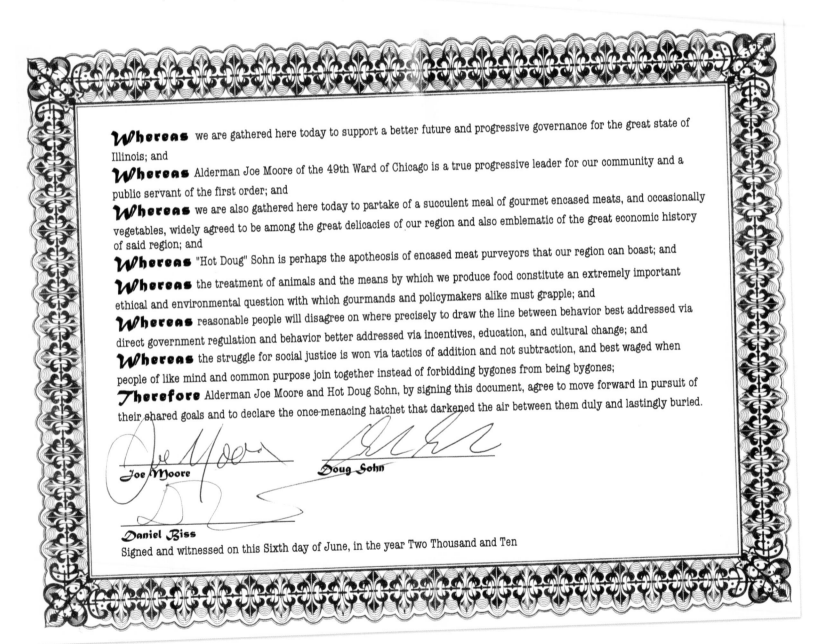

Whereas we are gathered here today to support a better future and progressive governance for the great state of Illinois; and

Whereas Alderman Joe Moore of the 49th Ward of Chicago is a true progressive leader for our community and a public servant of the first order; and

Whereas we are also gathered here today to partake of a succulent meal of gourmet encased meats, and occasionally vegetables, widely agreed to be among the great delicacies of our region and also emblematic of the great economic history of said region; and

Whereas "Hot Doug" Sohn is perhaps the apotheosis of encased meat purveyors that our region can boast; and

Whereas the treatment of animals and the means by which we produce food constitute an extremely important ethical and environmental question with which gourmands and policymakers alike must grapple; and

Whereas reasonable people will disagree on where precisely to draw the line between behavior best addressed via direct government regulation and behavior better addressed via incentives, education, and cultural change; and

Whereas the struggle for social justice is won via tactics of addition and not subtraction, and best waged when people of like mind and common purpose join together instead of forbidding bygones from being bygones;

Therefore Alderman Joe Moore and Hot Doug Sohn, by signing this document, agree to move forward in pursuit of their shared goals and to declare the once-menacing hatchet that darkened the air between them duly and lastingly buried.

Joe Moore

Doug Sohn

Daniel Biss

Signed and witnessed on this Sixth day of June, in the year Two Thousand and Ten

The great detente meeting of June 6, 2010. From let to right: some guy in a hot dog outfit, me, Illinois State Senator Daniel Biss, and Chicago Alderman Joe Moore. While it may not rival the great peace conferences in history, it still goes to prove that there is always hope for diplomacy and accord.

The Community

CHAPTER 7

Tattoos, T-Shirts, and Travel

Hot Doug's Fans

When I get asked "why don't you franchise?" my usual response is, "Why would I want more restaurants when I barely want one?" The real reason I only have one restaurant is that the part of the job I most enjoy I couldn't do if I had more than one. It's also the reason I take all of the orders: I genuinely enjoy taking care of the customers. I am constantly humbled and awed by the people who come in and about how passionate so many of them are about Hot Doug's. Seeing kids grow up, talking about travels, talking sports, talking concerts. OK, so there is the slight possibility that the reason the line can be so long is that there is a lot of talking going on. But, hey, it's my store and I like the talking. ¶ When we first asked for customer contributions for this book, I was hoping that we'd get a half-dozen or so. We may have surpassed that number just a bit. My heartfelt thanks go out to all of you who have not only contributed to the book, but who continue to come to Hot Doug's and let me try to make you laugh and feed you. It's a genuine honor.

The Tattoo Guarantee

One of my best customers at both the old store and the new one (I still like to call it "the new one," even though it's been open almost three times longer than the first store) is a former Lane Tech student by the name of Alex Baez. When he first started coming in, he was easy to notice because (a) he came in three or four times a week, and (b) he had a pointy mohawk à la Tim Armstrong of Rancid. He looked like every kid who hung out in front of the Dunkin' Donuts at Clark and Belmont in the nineties. (Medusa's anyone?)

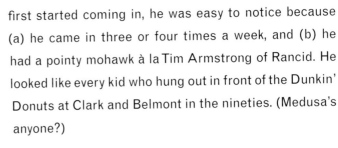

One day he comes in and shows me his new tattoo: the Hot Doug's logo guy on the inside of his arm, from elbow to wrist. My response, once the bewilderment wore off, was that there was simply no way he should ever pay for a hot dog again. And he hasn't.

Somehow, word spread about this. The tattoos started to trickle in. And then, thanks to a couple of tattoo blogs, as well as an article detailing the journey from tattoo parlor to Hot Doug's that appeared in the *Chicago Tribune*, it kind of exploded. As of this writing, there are almost 60 people with Hot Doug's tattoos. And while I'm a little creeped out, I'm way more flattered.

Alex Baez: The first Hot Doug's tattoo.

TATTOO TRENDSETTER

I believe it was 2008. Valentine's was around the corner and my girlfriend at the time mentioned getting me a tattoo as a gift. I was a budding music engineer/producer at that point so naturally ideas for my very first tattoo were music related. More specifically, a Smashing Pumpkins tat. I quickly realized that was lame and considered the next thing that means the world to me: food. Then I asked myself what my favorite food item was. Hot dogs. From where? You already know the answer to that!

The artist (Richard Dean) at that time was operating out of his kitchen so originally I was worried I would have a mangled wiener on my arm, but he did a great job! It hurt at some points and I was just looking at myself like, "Yo, you're getting a freakin' Hot Doug's tattoo bro! Is this a good idea?"

It was a great idea.

I still remember the first thing Doug said when I showed him the tat the next day: "Alex, that has got to be the most flattering, and also one of the creepiest, things I've ever seen in my life."

— ALEX "PAPA BEATZ" BAEZ

For you youngsters out there contemplating this, there are five rules about the tattoo:

1. **It has to feature the Hot Doug's character and say "Hot Doug's," whether in the banner or elsewhere. We also allow for artistic license, so it doesn't have to look exactly like our logo.**

2. **While I may not ask to see it each time you come in, if I do ask, you are required to show it to me. This may influence where on your person you decide to get inked. Or not.**

3. **It cannot be microscopic. I have to be able to see it and I've been wearing glasses since the first grade.**

4. **The tattoo does not allow you to jump the line. No matter where it is.**

5. **Remember: the tattoo is permanent; I am not. And I have an affinity for cured meats and Scotch. I'm just sayin'.**

PHOTO BY KINNIER LASTIMOSA

April Cheverette and Coleen Devanie with Doug.

After Doug confirmed that a Hot Doug's tattoo meant free dogs for life, we sat down to wait for our food and immediately called our friend Rich, who works around the corner at A+ tattoo studio. He fired up the tattoo machine and was ready to go by the time we had finished lunch and made our way over. April and I both chose to wear the logo with pride on our right wrists.

On April 5, 2010, April Cheverette became the eighth person to wear the logo permanently and I became the ninth person. I tried to talk Doug into calling me "Number Nine" after that, but for some reason he insists upon calling me Colleen. Since then, I have enjoyed countless free sausages and have loved every one of them. I love introducing friends and family to Hot Doug's and the conversations I can strike up with strangers, friends, and colleagues around our mutual love for Doug's ability to create the most amazing flavor combinations.

— **COLLEEN DEVANIE**

I recently got a tattoo of a hot dog dressed as a pinup girl, and I asked Doug whether he would put a photo of it on the wall. He said, "Certainly! However, you know if you get the Hot Doug's logo tattooed on you, you get free food for life." I looked at him in amazement and said, "Really?" He said, "Yes, but you have to get it some place I can see it."

I told my good friend Colleen, who is also a fan of Doug's, and we both thought this was a wonderful idea. The very next week we got matching tattoos. I was the eighth person and she was the ninth to have the Hot Doug's tattoo. It's on our wrists.

— **APRIL CHEVERETTE**

A.C. COVALSKY

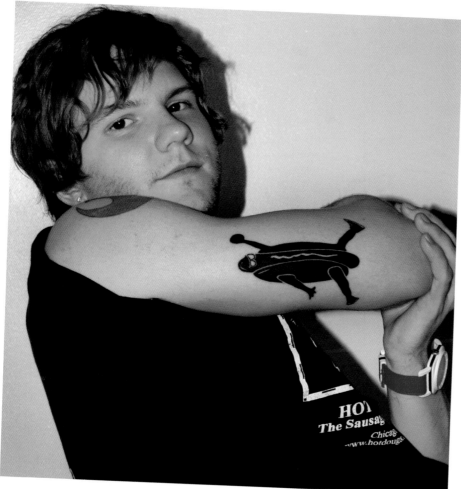

PAUL BUTTER

CHRISTIAN COVALSKY

Here is my Hot Doug's tattoo, on the back of my right calf/ankle. Dig!

—NICK KAMINSKY

JON WHITE

Free food or not, I fully embrace Doug's dedication and enthusiasm for wild encased meats, and am proud to sport such a fine institution on my arm! I would honestly trade free food for cuts in line though... — **JOSH DAVIS**

JASON S. THOMPSON

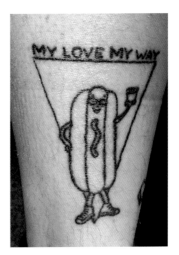

DAVE CRONIN

I've been to a lot of places and eaten a lot of hot dogs. There just isn't a better version of the dish than the one served in Chicago. Hot Doug's serves all the classic sausages and they do them well, and the buns and toppings are always fresh. Then you have the specials menu. You'd be hard-pressed to find a better meal served on a bun than the foie gras dog. When Doug said if I got his logo tattooed on me I would eat for free, there was no looking back. Shortly after, I was back at Hot Doug's with my new tattoo. Doug thanked me and said, "You get to eat here for free for the rest of your life. No wait, the rest of MY life." We laughed, I thanked him, and the rest is history. — **DEAN JOHNSON**

Work in progress.
— **JENNIFER JANACEK**

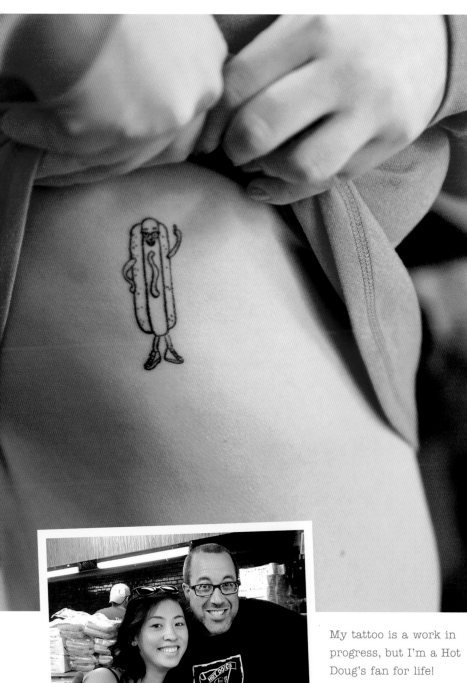

Whenever I go out of town to a rock show/music fest, I always like to represent Hot Doug's. Since I tend to see a lot of punk rock, this is a perfect choice because, let's face it, HD's is pretty rock in its own right. I was down in Austin this past weekend for Fun Fun Fun, and I ran across a guy who had a permanant tribute. Keep up the good work.

— DONALD ARQUETTE

My tattoo is a work in progress, but I'm a Hot Doug's fan for life!
— REBECCA FEDER

JOSH MILLER

ERIC ORR

When I started my sleeve of places I like to eat, I couldn't think of any other place to start with than Hot Doug's.

— **PATRICK McBRIDE**

This is a cross between the Hot Doug's logo and a Minor Threat t-shirt. It was very painful but worth every sausage.

— **LIAM O'DONNELL**

DOUG SAWYER

My first thought after eating Hot Doug's for the first time was, "How did I not know about this place sooner?!?" It didn't take long for it to become my favorite restaurant. Where else can you make your dining experience as simple or as complex as this? You can get a corn dog or foie gras. A Chicago dog with everything or a South African beef-and-pork boerwors with piri piri sweet mustard, caramelized onions, and mustard seed Gouda.

When I heard about the tattoo deal, I didn't hesitate (it's on my right calf, on the outside of my leg). Doug has always run his business in a personal, word-of-mouth fashion. You don't see ads or billboards for Hot Doug's, yet everybody knows what it is. What better way to celebrate this establishment than by getting a tattoo (a very personal art form)? — **JOSH MARKWARD**

I am 23 years old, I'm a costume designer and I have a Hot Doug's tattoo. My friend Speck at Mastermind did it in July of 2012, a year after I "broke veg." The duck also had to be in there. I'd like to think that every duck in the farm, once they learn they will be be part of a batch of Hot Doug's famous french fries, practically throw themselves into the grinder. At the time I got the tattoo, I had only been to HD's once, but I knew at first bite that there was no turning back. My mom was a little less than overjoyed, but once I get her in on the weekend for some duck fat fries, I know she'll be whistling a different tune. Between bites, that is.

— KATE GRUBE

SARAH GHORBANIAN

TATTOO EXTREME

Now, about rule #4 (page 177): One day a lovely young lady came to the front of the counter and told me she had gotten a **Hot Doug's** tattoo. I said thank you, and, as always, asked to see it. She paused for a moment, told me that she didn't want to show it to me right then, and handed me her iPhone, on which she had a photo of her tattoo. It was, uh, delicately located.

After trying not to (a) blush profusely, (b) literally swoon, or (c) lose complete composure, I took a knee until mustering the ability to speak. Then I told her that I would need to, at some point, see the actual tattoo (I'm not totally stupid). She told me I could whenever I was ready. I quickly replied, "Oh, I'll never be ready."

I finally saw it. I've got to say, it's the one and only time I actually felt like a rock star. But no, she does not get to jump the line.

(turn the page if you want...note: no one said this was a kid's book)

T-Shirts Around the World

After visiting Hot Doug's in 2009, my wife and I knew we would come back often for delicious sausage regardless of where we lived. We combined our love of food and travel by representing Hot Doug's during our trips to the Colosseum in 2010, Machu Picchu in 2011, and the Leaning Tower of Pisa in 2012.

—NICK FRASIER

This was submitted to us through Facebook and we couldn't figure out who it was or where these photos were taken. They're great photos, though. So thank you for the submission—and for sharing Hot Doug's with the elephant community.

I have been going to Hot Doug's about once a week, every week, for the last 5 or so years. In that time I have worn his shirt in various countries across the globe and had his logo tattooed permanently on my body. My friends and I have developed a personal relationship with Doug, to the point where he even officiated my friend's wedding. So with all that in mind, it's strange to think that my first Doug's experience came not of my own volition, but because I owed a favor to a friend who filled in on guitar for an old band of mine. To this day, it's the single greatest favor I have ever had to do for someone. If only all favors were, "You have to take me to Hot Doug's"! —**DAVE CRONIN**

Here's the pic I took wearing a Hot Doug's shirt at McMurdo Station, Antarctica. I believe it was taken in August, right before the first sunrise after the long dark winter. There was a massive snowstorm that day. The wind was blowing like 50 miles an hour or something, and the temperature with wind chill was like minus 95. Visibility was supposed to get down to just a few feet, and they were starting to string ropes in between buildings to help people walk. Needless to say, we should not have been outside, but I wanted to get a good shot for you.

—**MAX MILLER**

The Bourdain Effect

If you're me, and you're in my business, Anthony Bourdain is the guy. He's the man. If he says yours is the place to go, if he puts you on his TV show, you're golden. There are a lot of critics, and a lot of people I admire, but he's the guy.

So we've had a number of chefs and well-known people who've come in to the store. I've really never been starstruck. I'm excited to see people I recognize, but am always reserved and careful to treat a celebrity with the same respect I treat every other customer. It doesn't make me nervous. But the first time Anthony Bourdain came in (I believe he was in Chicago on a book tour—the show was on but it wasn't really big yet), it was about 11 a.m. on a weekday, it wasn't very crowded, and I didn't really notice him until he was behind the person whose order I was taking. And I looked up, saw him, and immediately my hands were shaking and my heart was pounding.

I'm pretty sure I said hello, I'm pretty sure I said I was honored to have him there. He ordered a Chicago hot dog and fries. I asked him if he wanted it steamed or grilled. He looked at me for the answer and I said grilled. I'm pretty sure the next seven to 10 people in line may or may not have gotten their order correctly. I have no recollection.

On the way out, he said, "That was great," and gave me a thumbs-up. For me, it was truly a great moment.

A few months later, someone from his show, *No Reservations*, called to tell me they were coming to Chicago and asked if they could film at Hot Doug's. Now I'm no believer of absolutes, and I always like to take time to ponder before answering questions. Not this time. Absolutely they could come film, no question about that. They asked if they could do it on a day we served duck fat fries—Friday or Saturday. If they couldn't have come on those days, I would have made an exception. (The list of people I would make this exception for is pretty slim: Anthony Bourdain, Madonna—alone, not with her people—and Joe Strummer, though he's no longer alive so the list is pretty short. And I'm not so sure about Madonna either.) They also wanted me to sit down with him for a conversation, which would've been difficult to do while we were open. I've got a business to run, you know. So I asked if we could do that part at the end of the day, after we closed. They were fantastic about that. They totally acquiesced to my schedule, came in late on a Friday afternoon, had a very small crew. Anthony waited in line. (When people complain about waiting in line, I get to say, "Well, Bourdain waited in line.")

It was just a great experience. They filmed it at the end of the summer in 2007. Anthony ordered a hot dog, duck fat fries, and the foie gras sausage. He was incredibly respectful of me and the restaurant. He ate, they filmed, we closed at 4. We had a little break while the crew got set up for the interview. We had a chance to chit-chat before they started filming. I was leaving for Sicily in a couple of months for vacation and I sheepishly asked him for recommendations. (He recommended the spleen sandwich at Antica Focacceria di San Francesco in Palermo, which was so good I had two.) We talked about foie gras, and then we sat down for the interview. I remember watching the show when it aired in February 2008, and I have to say I was fairly impressed that I sounded pretty coherent, considering that the only thing going through my head at that time was, "How is this humanly possible?" This was truly one of the best experiences I've had at the restaurant. He couldn't have been cooler, he was great with the staff

TORONTO: 900 MILES, THREE TIMES IN THREE YEARS

"An idea. Resilient, highly contagious. Once an idea has taken hold of the brain it's almost impossible to eradicate. An idea that is fully formed, fully understood—that sticks. Right in there, somewhere." —Cobb (played by Leonardo DiCaprio, *Inception*)

This happened to me one fateful Toronto afternoon in 2009 as I was watching TV. I was watching Anthony Bourdain visit Chicago, where he stopped by this nondescript sausage place. The scene ended with me thinking, "OK, I need to go there." I loved the idea of taking something so common, such as a sausage, and just making it your own—while not charging an arm and a leg for it. Even better is that the place is a no-frills, friendly joint. And so I took eight friends with me to Chicago, specifically to eat at Hot Doug's. And then two more friends in 2011 and again just a couple of weeks ago! That's 5,400 km (or 7,000,000 miles, I think) of driving just to savor what Chicago gets to eat every single day.

In 2010, I told Doug I was from Toronto to which he replied, "Tell Hedo Turkoglu he ruined my basketball pool." I did, and next season he left the Raptors. Thanks, Doug.

—JEFF CHAN, TORONTO

LOCAL PERSPECTIVE

I have been frequenting this establishment for many years, back before all the cable food shows discovered our secret gem, and before the travel guides listed him as one of just a few places worth visiting in Chicago. Yes, a couple things are different now; mostly, you have to go at about 10:30 (right when the doors open) to avoid the daily two- to three-hour lines, but what hasn't changed is the excellent food and the outstanding personal service that each and every person gets directly from Doug.

Each and every person who comes in has the pleasure of ordering directly from the man himself. Where else are you going to have personal one-on-one time with the chef of a gourmet restaurant, every single time you come in? It is truly a joy to talk and joke and catch up with Doug whenever I'm lucky enough to stop by, and I highly encourage everyone to stop by and meet my friend Doug for yourself. The experience will change your life.

— **JOSHUA HELLE**

and the other customers, taking photos with everyone. When someone you genuinely admire turns out not to be a jackass, it's totally great.

When the show finally aired, it coincided within a couple of months of another Travel Channel show called *Hot Dog Paradise*. To this day, the Travel Channel continues to air both episodes (God bless them). We were doing just fine prior to that, but these shows took us to the next level. We quickly discovered the fervor of Anthony's fans and just how devoted they are. Wherever he recommends, people go. Which I totally get—I do the same thing. I make notes of the places I want to visit based on what he says. It was not only the reaction of people from Chicago, but this incredible worldwide effect. He's a popular fella—people still, to this day, come in to the restaurant because they saw it on his show. I owe a great deal of thanks to him for the financial success of the restaurant.

I'm also really proud that we are now listed in guide books all around the world—it's pretty damn cool. About a year ago, we had a young couple from Korea come in, and they had a copy of *Lonely Planet Chicago*, which I took a look at—a bunch of Korean characters, and then "Hot Doug's." Not bad.

I always used to think: Really? You're in downtown Chicago and you're going to trek out here? And then I think, well yeah, that's exactly what I would do too. When the G8 summit was in Chicago in 2012, we had several dignitaries from foreign countries come in with their department attachés. It's amazing how many foreign travelers will come to a restaurant that is quite inconveniently located, has bad hours, and closes randomly for no apparent reason.

Also, for some weird reason we're apparently huge in South America.

My heartfelt thanks to Anthony Bourdain for coming to see us. Oh, and if I may brag a bit, we're pretty proud of the fact that we're on the list of his 13 restaurants to go to before you die (and there are actually real restaurants on that list!).

"YOU GOT IT!"

Whenever my family from out of town visits, they want to go to places that can only be found in Chicago. Expensive sit-down restaurants make them uncomfortable—I knew Alinea or Next was out of the question—so I thought Hot Doug's would be the perfect place for lunch. They were getting antsy during the wait, but as soon as they got to the front and heard Doug's catchphrase ("You got it!"), they were overjoyed.

— JENNY SIKORA

Top left: The Dog and the Paul Kelly; top right: that's me, eating the Dave Pound; bottom, from left to right: me (Jenny Sikora), Doug, Lina Sikora, Angie Motivar, and my dad, Eugene Sikora.

PENNSYLVANIA VISITORS

My boyfriend, his daughter, and I recently traveled to Chicago from Pennsylvania, and we all experienced our first Chicago-style hot dog at Hot Doug's. Without a doubt, it was one of the most amazing and delicious food items I've ever put in my mouth! We initially saw your restaurant on Anthony Bourdain's *No Reservations* and marked it down as one of the places we'd take the time to visit when in the Windy City...and we're so glad we did! It was definitely worth the taxi ride out of downtown, and worth standing an hour in 90-degree weather. Everyone was so friendly and welcoming. There were certainly lots of customers waiting patiently like us, so for the staff at Hot Doug's to be as kind and sociable as they were the entire time was impressive. They came to check on us outside to make sure we weren't melting away, and offered water if we needed it. You certainly don't get that at any other encased-meat joints :) Once inside, we had the greatest experience.

— KARLA BETTS

FROM DC TO OAK PARK TO CALIFORNIA AVE

I'm from the DC area, and when my wife told me we were going to Chicago I had a relatively short to-do list: Hot Doug's.

That July was sweltering hot—I'm talking triple digits. We were in Oak Park at the Frank Lloyd Wright House when I saw it was close to 2:30. We grabbed a cab ($40) and took our place in line. Someone else in line passed out and had to be taken away in an ambulance. They brought out the hose to keep us from dehydrating. And still, we waited. We must've been in line for 90 minutes. Finally we get in and we go for it. I get the duck sausage with foie gras and the Celebrity Sausage: a spicy little crawfish number with smoked cheese, named after another of George Clooney's lovely exes, as Doug was proud to point out. We topped it off, naturally, with some duck fat fries. Holy cow. I've never had anything like it before or since, and I doubt I will until I'm back on California Ave.

After managing to savor my meal instead of devouring it like a rabid dog, I go up to Doug at the counter. By this time the line is closed, and I tell him, "Look, I flew out from DC yesterday. Took a $40 cab ride to wait in one of the longest lines I've ever waited in, on one of the hottest days I can remember."

At this point Doug gets this look that says, "Oh great, this tourist is going to let me have it."

I finish with, "And I'd do it all over again tomorrow. That was phenomenal." He gives us a smile, a gracious "thanks," and a handshake. We depart, and I spend the rest of the weekend chasing the dragon that is the food high one gets upon a visit to Hot Doug's.

— **JOSH BROHAWN**

AUSSIE TRANSPLANT

After years as a regular at Hot Doug's, I hit my life's reset button in 2007 and moved to Australia. During the years since, several Aussie friends have asked me for advice when planning a holiday in Chicago. My responses always include a visit to Hot Doug's.

Their trip to Avondale plays out something like this in my mind: Jokes are made at first sight of the queue, followed by a short discussion of the sanity of joining it. Curiosity wins; and once in line, conversation with the regulars exposes them to a part of the city's soul most tourists would miss. Forty-seven minutes pass before their audience with the Meat Oracle, where the decision is surprisingly difficult. Preconceived notions of a "hot dog lunch" vanish at first glance of the menu. Indecision wins, and an embarrassing amount of food is ordered. They eat it all. Eyes glance around the store, from the décor to the patrons, then to Doug. It starts to all make sense. On the way out, a nod and smile are exchanged with the regulars still in line; a silent admission that yes, my friends, it is indeed worth it.

Back home, I'm told of a great holiday made even better, accompanied by the inevitable photo of a brick building on a street corner in Avondale, from which a line of people 30 feet long patiently waits. I too nod and smile, knowing how much I miss being in that line.

Char Brat. Cheese. Caramelized onions. Mr. Pibb. — **CURTIS MALASKY**

BELGIAN TRAVELERS

My girlfriend and I are from Belgium and were visiting our friend Paul Suwan. We had a great time and some excellent food!

—SAMUEL LETECHEUR

A VERY SPECIAL FOOD TRIP TO CHICAGO

I wanted to share with you a quick story about my mother and her trip to Chicago. My mom and sisters moved away from the Chicago suburbs to Austin, TX, in 1998 and she has only been back a few times since. I alone stayed in the Chicago area. In 2010, my mother came into town to do a "foodie" tour. She went to many well-known and upscale establishments but one place she really wanted to visit was Hot Doug's. On that Friday morning we were ready to wait outside in the rain for a long time to get those amazing duck fat fries, but unfortunately my mother wasn't feeling so well. In an effort to make sure she still had her fix we waited outside, in the rain, for over an hour for her. We ordered over eight different things plus fries to make sure she had a nice sam-

pling. We drove downtown to her hotel and had a picnic right there with some amazing food. Her favorite, of course, was the duck sausage. She was in heaven!

After my mom's amazing trip to Chicago she went home to find out her aches and pains were actually lung cancer. She was diagnosed with stage IV—it was in her kidneys, lungs, and spine. It was a very painful type of cancer, which is why we are thankful she didn't have to suffer that long. She passed on December 30, 2010.

One of my talks with my mom about her life came back to her last trip to Chicago. She was so thankful for having gone and done everything she wanted to do. We visited her grandparents' old homes and learned about lost family history.

She had me drive her around town to visit her old neighborhood and even met some long lost relatives. Of course, the best part was the food. Chicago is a great food city and we enjoyed so much of it. I am very thankful that she was able to enjoy her Hot Doug's even if she couldn't visit the restaurant itself. It was the icing on the cake for a great last trip that she was able to enjoy.

I wanted to share my mother's story so people can understand the impact Hot Doug's had on her trip to Chicago. Eating isn't just a source of energy but something we can enjoy and do together. It makes memories and I will never forget the days I spent in Chicago with her.

—DEB MONKMAN

MAINE: 17 HOURS...PLUS 1

My boyfriend, Steve Sidelinger, is a chef at a restaurant called Hot Suppa' in Portland, Maine. We met in January 2011, and from the beginning, he spoke of wanting to go to your restaurant. The owners of Hot Suppa' traveled the USA before opening their restaurant, and they collected many menus from all over. Steve read about Hot Doug's on the back of the employee bathroom door, and knew he had to make the trip. For our birthdays, we planned our entire first vacation together around going to Hot Doug's. We took the trip May 2011, and drove straight from Portland to Chicago, straight to Hot Doug's for lunch. His quote: "The 17-hour drive plus 1 hour in line was well worth the wait." We loved the food, the atmosphere, and the fact that Doug took our order! Steve is already dying to go back but he wishes he could get delivery to Maine even more! — **JOCELYN FRENCH**

TURKEY TOURISTS

In January of 2008, I was in Istanbul, Turkey, on vacation—far away from the imperial palace of encased meats on California and Roscoe. I met an American author who said that after her divorce was final, she was moving back to Chicago.

"What do you miss about Chicago?" I asked.

"The food! There was this one hot dog place called..." At that point I sort of dismissed her and said, "When you come to Chicago, I'm taking you to Hot Doug's."

That summer, I introduced her to Hot Doug's, which she so strongly approved of that Hot Doug's became a weekend "treat" we'd prepare for days in advance. On the day her book launched, Doug was gracious enough to give her the prestigious title of Celebrity Sausage—a surprise that I hope was way more of a life-changer than the birth of her child, her graduation from college, her marriage, or her book deal. I mean, what's the big deal about motherhood anyway?

Over the years, Hot Doug's was an experience shared with her friends and family. Her new husband, a British gentleman, realized that the sausages he ate all his life in England were mere imitations compared to the culinary cuisine that Hot Doug's can create. For him, Chicago means a new wife, a great city, and encased meats. Now the British know why we declared independence from them. And quite frankly, if her husband didn't like Hot Doug's, I would have said he's no good. And probably had him deported. — **NICK HAWKINS**

SOUTHERN HOSPITALITY

I was visiting a friend who had just moved to Chicago from Dallas, and both of us were dying to try Hot Doug's. It was December and getting out and about was a pain for us Southern girls, but we prevailed. Upon arrival we discovered a line, and after waiting for a bit we also discovered it was cash only. After putting together the few sad dollar bills we had between us, and adding in some parking meter change from the bottom of our purses, we established a budget and worked out what we could order. By the time we got to the counter we were laughing about our unfortunate circumstances. We'd been dying to come, and now that we had arrived we could only share a hot dog and some fries. (We had wanted to order several to try them all!)

Doug himself was behind the counter, and we were starstruck. He overheard our conversation and asked us what we'd order if we weren't limited by our own ignorance of the cash-only rule. He said, "Pay what you can and the rest is on me." What a guy! I thoroughly enjoyed our visit and will definitely go back every time I'm in Chicago!

—**SHANNA LEE**

FIRST TRIP: EAT THIS!

Even before my first remarkable trip there in 2005, my friend Kristin spoke of Hot Doug's as one speaks of a pilgrimage site. Back in summer 2005, Kristin and I were graduate students, and we had signed up to work as volunteers at an elementary school on the far south side. Being relatively new to Chicago and green regarding the city traffic, we did not allow ourselves enough time to make a long drive. Anyway, at 9:30 a.m. when we were supposed to be reporting at the school, we found ourselves stuck on Belmont still trying to get onto Lakeshore Drive. To make a long story short, we called our supervisor, who let us off lightly, and we turned back to Kristin's apartment to study. An hour later, Kristin had the bright idea that we should go to Hot Doug's. Although the idea of eating lunch so early was a little strange to me, we went. Imagine

it—my first visit—and the Food Network was there interviewing Doug for a new show called *Eat This!* Dave Lieberman, the host of the show, invited Kristin and me, the only guests at 10.30 a.m. on a Monday, to eat with him and talk about all five sausages Doug had served him. We got to eat free delicious food and talk about the free delicious food! It was a dream, and Hot Doug's became legendary to me. Hot Doug's is a cornerstone of Kristin's and my friendship. Whenever we have the odd holiday from work we eat there. Long weekday lines sure beat really long weekend lines. Although our new mayor is cracking down on the number of holidays that hardworking CPS employees receive, and our lives are busy and it can be difficult to meet up, Kristin and I meet at Hot Doug's regularly. Doug knows us by name, and it's a comfortable feeling to go and eat there. And now Kristin's baby joins us, wiggling merrily in his baby carrier! Hot Doug's is a symbol of my life in Chicago, and I agree that it's a pilgrimage site! —**LAURA G.**

CALIFORNIA DREAMIN'

My relationship with Hot Doug's goes back to the fall of 2005 when, as a freshly minted resident doctor at the University of Chicago, I met Doug's dad, urologist Dr. Herb Sohn. He told me proudly that his son had

a hot dog restaurant that had been featured in *Bon Appétit*. Of course, he also told me all sorts of wild tales about riding in a helicopter with former President Clinton, and starting his own private medical school, so I had written him off as a bit of a demented old man. When I realized Hot Doug's DID exist, I talked a number of my colleagues into skipping out of work to try it for lunch. Twice. Both times, Doug was on vacation and no hot dogs were had.

Over the next four years, Chicago became my home. I loved the intensity and the honesty of it. I loved the neighborhoods and the beauty

of living there. I loved its people, so brash and welcoming at the same time. When it came time to move west for my next job, my friends and I started working through the list of must-do activities that make Chicago Chicago, and that made me a Chicagoan. And so it was in late June 2009 when my friends and I played hooky from work and made our first successful trip to Hot Doug's. The line was long, even at 10 a.m., but BYO champagne in hand, we were ready to pay the price for glory.

I only remember one of the six sausages we had that day, the BLT, a gorgeous, silky link of smoked back bacon with cherry tomatoes and a basil aioli, but I'll always remember Doug's warm welcome and the great time my friends and I had reminiscing about our time in Chicago and lamenting it had taken us that long to get to Doug's. It was the best sausage I'd ever had, and although I still check the online menu for it from time to time, I haven't seen it since.

We rounded out the day with a behind-the-scenes tour of Wrigley Field, a visit to the top of the Hancock for a view of all the places

I'd been and seen in my four years there, and drinks with friends in the evening.

I left Chicago for San Francisco, but I never forgot Hot Doug's. Northern California may be a culinary hot spot, but the state of high-end encased meats is deplorable. I wear my red Hot Doug's t-shirt to the gym, to the climbing gym, and out running, and I've been stopped at least a half-dozen times by friends of the restaurant. Everyone who's tried it loves it, and anyone who could recognize a Hot Doug's t-shirt ended up being a pretty cool person. I've been back to Doug's twice since that first time, once on a visit with Chicago friends, and once with the girl I'm going to marry. She's a product of Northern California and although she loves a good sausage, her tastes are, how should I say it, overly organic?

I planned out our first trip to Chicago designed to impress: world-class museums, tours of Lincoln Park, parties with friends, concerts of my favorite bands, dinner at Michelin-star restaurants, and drinks at the chicest lounges. And as great as all that was, and despite how early we had to get up and how ridiculous she thought we were when we first ended up in line, she still says her favorite part of the trip was the Game of the Week (smoked yak), the duck fat fries, and the hospitality at Doug's. —**CHRIS CHOUKALAS**

I'M GOING TO LET YOU IN ON A LITTLE SECRET: THE SMELL OF SAUSAGE COOKING ON A CHAR GRILL IS MIGHTY MIGHTY FINE. IT LOOKS PRETTY COOL, TOO.

SAUSAGE
MR & MRS RULLO
$7.50
Taco Pork Sausage
with Green Chili Mayonnaise
and Queso Asadero
Spicy Jack Cheese-Stuffed Pork Sausage
with Spicy Passion Fruit Mayonnaise
and Habanero Jack Cheese

CHAPTER 8

Hook-ups, Break-ups, Engagements & Marriages

Connecting Through Hot Doug's

Although it's the one aspect of the Hot Doug's experience I'm the least familiar with, I do have a small inkling of what it's like to be a customer at my restaurant. Like my customers, I travel a lot and go far out of my way for a unique dining experience. I also enjoy the feeling of knowing I'm sharing something with a group of like-minded souls. I can't overstate the joy, flattery, and feelings of humility I experience seeing both familiar and new faces at Hot Doug's. The humanity of this shared experience is keenly intriguing to me. Friendships have been forged, laughs have been shared, stories have been traded in line, at the counter, and at the tables. Oh, and there has been more than one marriage proposal (ah, the magic of sausage). Here are just a few of the stories.

Nothing Says Love Like Sausage

A HOT DOUG'S ROMANCE BY SHANNON RULLO

To most of the world, Hot Doug's is simply a tasty sausage emporium that occasionally has marathon-long lines. For my husband Pete and myself, over the years Hot Doug's hasn't just become a weekly life choice; it's been the scene of a first date, an unexpected proposal, and a wedding hosted by the Sausage King himself.

I'm a stalker's dream. For the past two years, every Monday around the same time, you will find me eagerly standing in line at Hot Doug's. Now before you think I'm super boring, prior to that it was every Wednesday. There's a little wildness in this soul after all! Luckily for me, I happened to find the one man in this big city we call Chicago who I could not only tolerate, but who also had a Monday Hot Doug's routine as strict as mine. So where do two blossoming lovebirds go to conquer the dreaded first date? Hot Doug's, duh! What, did you think I was going to say Olive Garden or something?

I remember it like it was yesterday: a warm summer's day, and the usual annoyances of muggy air and tourist

line didn't seem to bother me as much. If you are unfamiliar with "tourist line," it is the line that, instead of wrapping safely around the Hot Doug's building on Roscoe, trickles into oncoming traffic on California. I personally don't like to get hit by cars before I eat tasty food, but apparently a lot of people visiting Hot Doug's do. Who knew? Regardless, Cupid's wizardry was in the air, and I was smitten.

Fast-forward to what I assumed was a basic Monday sausage extravaganza. Little did I know that this Monday would turn out to be more than a Game-of-the-Week kind of day. We approached the counter, and in typical fashion began to catch up with Doug. The only difference: as the words for my order came out my mouth, Pete suddenly acted as if he had forgotten his money. A second later, he was on his knee and a ring was in my face. I was in shock! The poor man tried to utter some words from a speech he had nervously planned, and all I could do was repeatedly tell him to shut up. I of course said yes, people clapped, and I'm pretty sure someone kissed a baby.

The week to follow was a whirlwind. Our engagement story was plastered on the cover of the *Chicago Tribune*, featured on various websites, and spot-

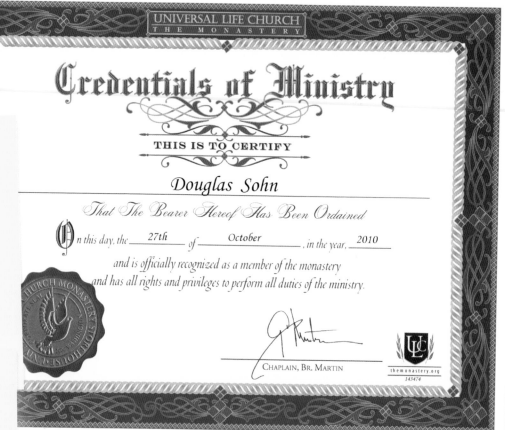

UNLIKE MANY OF THE HOT DOUG'S STORIES OUT THERE, ME OFFICIATING SHANNON AND PETE'S WEDDING CEREMONY IS TRUE (FOR THE RECORD: I AM NOT MARRIED TO THE OWNER OF THE HAIR SALON NEXT TO THE FIRST HOT DOUG'S). AS

AN ORDAINED MINISTER OF THE UNIVERSAL LIFE CHURCH MONASTERY (I THINK THAT ONE CAME UP FIRST ON GOOGLE), I MIGHT HAVE EVEN LEGALLY MARRIED THEM. EITHER WAY, THEY ARE A LOVELY COUPLE AND I IMMEDIATELY RETIRED FROM THE WEDDING OFFICIATING BUSINESS RIGHT AFTER THEIR SERVICE.

lighted on WCIU's *You and Me this Morning*. On top of all of that, Pete and I had wanted to get married on Halloween. The only problem was that Halloween was just a week away, and the idea of putting the wedding off for another year kind of made me want to vomit, *Exorcist*-style. Luckily for me, Pete had already spoken to Doug about getting ordained to officiate our wedding. To him, Doug and Hot Doug's had played a big part in both our lives over the years and it only seemed appropriate. Luckily for Pete, I agreed.

On October 31, 2010, Pete and I were married at the Metro concert hall. Doug officiated the ceremony in witty Doug-like fashion. It was everything a girl could ask for—and then some. This past year we celebrated our one-year anniversary with, of course, a pit stop at Hot Doug's. As our second anniversary quickly approaches, I'm sure we will keep the tradition going.

THANKS FOR THE HOOK-UP, EX

My ex-boyfriend introduced me to Hot Doug's over three years ago, when his dad saw it on the Travel Channel and insisted we go (seeing as we live in Chicago). This became our "special spot" when we wanted to grab a bite, just the two of us. Fast-forward three years, I have a new boyfriend, and this was one spot that I REFUSED to stop going to just because it brought back memories of relationships past. The current boyfriend received a different version of this story, which of course eliminates the ex altogether. Best part of all this: the current boyfriend loves Hot Doug's too, and after being introduced to it by me, thinks I'm a hip chick for knowing about a spot like Hot Doug's. I guess you can say, "And they all lived happily ever after." (Let's hope the ex did, too.)

— CHRIS DAVILA

SAUSAGE + BUBBLY = LOVE

One of my all-time favorite memories is from 2010, when my friends wanted to celebrate my recent engagement to my now-husband. So we gathered together to brave the long summer line. Friends brought wedding magazines, the fiancé and I brought champagne. After ordering all of our special sausages—always, always foie gras for my now-husband, along with at least one other—we toasted our engagement. The meal there with about 10 of our friends was our engagement party, and we still have the champagne cork to this day. — ELIZABETH SANFILIPPO

GROOM'S LUNCH DISASTER AVERTED

I got married in October of 2008. My wife and I are both from Detroit, but we moved to Chicago in our late teens/early 20s and made it our home. It was important for us to share our favorite parts of Chicago with our guests over the course of our wedding weekend. I discovered Hot Doug's in early 2005 and had become a regular visitor—so having an event at Doug's was a must.

We decided to hold our groom's lunch there with all the men in the wedding party the morning of the ceremony. I arrived at 10:15 and was one of the first in line with my 10 or so supporters behind me. The photographer was supposed to meet us there, but at 10:30, when the doors opened, she was nowhere to be found. She did not have a map to the next spot and I did not have a cell phone on me. I started freaking out. She was a new friend who had agreed to help us out, but we didn't really know her all that well. I thought she might have bailed when something better came up.

When I entered the friendly yellow, red, and blue confines, I saw her. Doug had let her in early to get our picture as we entered. In addition to setting up the scene he also comped a large portion of the lunch. I went from freaking out to being overwhelmed with gratitude. I have been to Hot Doug's almost 100 times over the past seven-plus years. I love the food; it's unique and delicious. But Doug's community on Roscoe and California is why I come back time and time again. — ROB RODEMEYER

Doug, Kev Dennis (the Bachelor), Tom Galateo (brother-in-law), and Mike Dennis (brother).

BACHELOR PARTY TO REMEMBER

It was the fall of 2003. Steve Bartman was on the lam, Hot Doug's was still located on Roscoe Street, and Kevin John Dennis was about to get married. Besides the birth of his sons and marrying the love of his life, Laura, one of the best events in Kev's life was his bachelor party at Hot Doug's.

Yes, that's right. A bachelor party at Hot Doug's.

We showed up wearing fake mustaches and giant cardboard hats. We requested that Doug make his special wild boar sausage and duck fat french fries. The night was pretty priceless, as we had the whole place (and Doug) to ourselves.

A few weeks later, my brother and I visited Hot Doug's and spotted a fake mustache on one of the infamous Elvis pictures. We both just chuckled.

In August 2009, we lost Kevin to an undetectable heart defect. Whenever Kev and his friends got together, they always reminisced about the bachelor party that took place at the Encased Meats Emporium and Sausage Superstore. This is a picture from the bachelor party. Some guys like Vegas; other guys just like a good hot dog. Thanks for the memories Doug. — **MIKE DENNIS**

ANNIVERSARY AT HOT DOUG'S

Our wedding anniversary is February 16th. In 2008, we planned a long-weekend degustation trip to Chicago to celebrate. I had given my husband a copy of the book *My Last Supper: 50 Great Chefs and Their Final Meals*, by Melanie Dunea; we were going to try to eat in every restaurant featured in the book and have each featured chef autograph it.

One night we ate at the chef's table at Charlie Trotter's; the next night we ate at Blackbird. If you have ever eaten at Blackbird, you know that the tables are very close together. Some of the other diners saw our book and asked about it. We explained what we were doing and the people sitting on both sides of us said, "You must add Hot Doug's to your list!" We had never heard of Hot Doug's, but all the diners around us said it had the best hot dogs, and if we went on Saturday, we could also get the absolute best french fries because they were fried in duck fat.

So, the next morning, we got up and hailed a cab from our downtown hotel and instructed the driver to take us to Hot Doug's. It was about a 40-minute drive one way and cost about $40—we were looking at $80 round-trip! When we arrived, there was already a line around the building, in spite of piles of snow and the temperature hovering around freezing. We got in line and were surprised to find out that some of our fellow line-goers were from the same area in Virginia as we are. They were a group of lawyers who were volunteering with then-Senator Obama's presidential campaign. What are the chances that you go to a small restaurant in a city 900 miles away and find someone from your hometown, standing in the same line? It all just added to the experience! We waited about half an hour and finally got our turn at the counter. We ordered our Chicago-style hot dogs and french fries. The whole bill was around $11. We had spent about $1,000 for dinner at Charlie Trotter's, and I have to say the value of the Hot Doug's lunch was better! Everything the other Blackbird diners had said about the food at Hot Doug's was true. It was worth it to stand in line in the middle of February. The whole experience was an adventure that we still talk about whenever our wedding anniversary rolls around each February.

—JOYCE MILLER AND
ALAN GAVALYA

DRESS STILL FITS!

My first Hot Doug's experience coincided with the day I picked up my wedding dress.

It was late June of 2009 when my wedding dress came in and of course I wanted to pick it up as soon as possible. My mom, sisters, and girlfriends were not available, so I called the next best thing: my best guy friend, a.k.a. my eating buddy and our "minister" for the wedding; he used to call me his "meat girlfriend" when his wife was still a vegetarian (yes, he converted her to our ways). Being the stand-up guy that he is, he agreed to come with me, under one condition: that we go to Hot Doug's first.

We arrived around 10:30 a.m. and of course there was a line, but it wasn't so bad. In the end we waited about 45 minutes. I think he ordered the bacon sausage; we both ordered the duck sausage with foie gras pâté, plus one to go for the fiancé. I couldn't resist also ordering a jalapeño pork sausage. Upon my first bite I knew that the duck sausage with the foie gras would be my favorite at Hot Doug's forever. It was soooo delicious; the foie was the perfect complement to the duck sausage. We also ordered duck fat fries—hello!—absolute deliciousness.

The two in the front: duck sausage with black truffle aioli and foie gras pâté on top; back left: bacon sausage; back right: smoky pork sausage with jalapeno cheese in the center.

I can't believe I ordered two sausages, but I couldn't have him order two and not match him. I think after our meal I had to walk around the block several times.

Every experience at Hot Doug's has been fabulous. Love everything I've tried.

And the dress fit perfectly. —ANNIE MARK KOS

IT'S A BOY! *AND A* HOT DOUG'S MIRACLE!

In the midst of the wonderful insanity of my son's birth, I didn't get much of a chance to eat—who's thinking about food when they're busy thinking about dilation and contractions, not to mention worrying like crazy? But after the storm of delivery had passed and my wife, son, and I were ensconced in a recovery room, hunger hit me hard. (Dads, in case you didn't know, aren't patients at hospitals, and are thus spared the indignity of hospital food.)

By the time my in-laws arrived from Milwaukee, I was as hungry as I'd ever been, a sensation that came not only from having not eaten, but from the tremendous relief of a birth without many bumps. I barely remember the drive from Swedish Covenant Hospital to Hot Doug's; I only remember that I was blearily frustrated that California Avenue—home to both Hot Doug's and the hospital—gets cut off in between them. Encased meat, so close and yet so far away.

My father-in-law, who was a first-timer, and I walked in to what I like to call the "Hot Doug's miracle"—that almost-unbelievable occasion when there's absolutely no line. Unshowered, sweat-panted, and mouth watering, I ordered for both of us. I don't remember what. It doesn't matter, because everything Doug serves is fantastic. I remember feeling like that first bite was the end of this giving-birth thing, or maybe it just felt like a nice respite. As always, that first bite felt satisfying in a way that few other foods ever do. Our boy, Jasper, who's now two and a half, has been to Hot Doug's a couple of times now, and he'll be a regular soon enough. He calls it "the hot dog ress-e-saunt," and he likes the veggie dogs. He also, like everybody else who makes the trek and braves the line, instinctively likes Doug. **— JOSH MODELL**

Birthdays at Hot Doug's

IT'S YOUR BIRTHDAY, YOU'RE A GYRO SAUSAGE

A few years back, my friend Cecile had somehow convinced Doug to make me the Celebrity Sausage of the Week as a birthday surprise. When I arrived at Hot Doug's on a cold wintery day, I only had deliciousness on my mind. I had absolutely NO idea that I would be a sausage!

My then-boyfriend had brought a weirdo picture of me, and Doug signed it, "Keep up the good work." It was the most incredible and wonderful day!

Since then, we moved to California, we got married, and my name has changed. Yet when we go back to Hot Doug's the one or two times a year we can, he still remembers me by name. (He also still refuses to come back to California with me.)

— JAMIE (MILLER) BLEICHNER

BIRTHDAY SURPRISE FOR HUBBY

In 2009, my husband Michael planned the greatest birthday surprise I can possibly imagine. For months he had been saving money to fly my entire immediate family out to Chicago from Reno, NV, for my 29th birthday. Now, we're not well off. I mean, I work in theater for crying out loud, so for him to plan this trip took a lot of sneaking around and hiding funds. I've never been happier to be deceived! As soon as I saw my family, I knew there was one thing in Chicago I needed them to experience: HOT DOUG'S! The late April weather was a bit chilly, but nobody complained about the wait because they'd heard us talk about the joy that is Doug's food. Needless to say, food was devoured, t-shirts were purchased, and our visit to Hot Doug's is still something we talk about on a regular basis. — **TYLER DEAN KEMPF**

Tyler Dean Kempf, niece Rhaegan, and husband/party planner Michael Deming.

Dennis Kempf, Tyler's father.

A TWO-YEAR OLD'S BIRTHDAY WISH

My family visited Chicago over spring break last year, which happened to fall on my daughter's second birthday. We gave her the choice of celebrating her special day at the American Girl store, or at Hot Doug's for what we called a "sausage party." She picked the sausage party! She enjoyed tastes of several kinds of sausages, along with her own red hot, and some duck fat fries. It was a great way to celebrate her birthday; her love of sausages continues. — **KATIE McCLARREN**

My husband, Ryan, and the birthday girl, Flannery.

Holidays and Special Memories

HOLIDAY FAMILY TRADITION

Coming from a fairly large extended family, it is difficult to spend quality time with everyone during the holidays. What we can ALL agree on is our annual pilgrimage to Hot Doug's. Our tradition goes something like this: The day or two before Christmas we meet at my house around noon, eat a small snack, and head out to the encased meat hall of fame to see Doug. That's right, we leave at noon, prime time for the monster line—several blocks of Hot Doug's fans packing the sidewalk, like the place is a methadone clinic on Free Drugs Day. We clamber out of our cars and assemble to begin the wait—and here is where this tradition gets cool.

With nothing to do but wait in line, we talk. Catch up. Make jokes and get joked about. In short, we act as a family. A happy, increasingly hungry, non-nuclear modern family, who milks the line at Hot Doug's for more than just the great food. We do it for love and for the ability to catch up without Twitter, Facebook, or whatever social network is popular this second. Doug, thank you, thanks to your staff, and thanks to all of the other fans out there who make the wait about more than just something to eat. YOU ROCK.

—KEVIN McCONKEY

REMEMBERING SEAN

My brother Sean passed away five years ago from a rare form of cancer. Sean knew about Hot Doug's way before anyone else did. He knew about it before being a foodie and finding the next great Chicago food joint was the popular thing to do, before any of the hundreds of write-ups it has received over the years. He came across Hot Doug's when we worked at Tower Records, and he turned his friends and family into dedicated, line-waiting customers. When we have family in town, Hot Doug's is a must. "It was Sean's favorite place," we tell them. It has become a place where my family and extended family meet, all because of Sean telling us around 10 years ago about this not-so-average hot dog joint. Some of my friends think the whole waiting in line thing is a joke, just for a hot dog? But it's not just a hot dog place for the Silvers, it's a place where we meet and we feel like Sean is there with us. **—BRIAN SILVER**

WHO'S ASKIN'?

My first journey to the castle of encased sausages was in winter 2007. I lived an hour away at the time, but my friend Derek had talked me into experiencing how delicious the food was. When I arrived, I was mesmerized by the bright red and yellow colors, splashed with celebrity photos and hot dog art. As I approached the register, this gentleman in thick-rimmed glasses says, "How are you doing, my friend?"

I asked: "Are you Doug?"

He replied: "Are you the cops?"

I shake my head. "No, not at all."

Doug smiled. "Hi, I'm Doug!"

You always remember your first time and I had a rattlesnake sausage that day with duck fat fries!

—DAVID C. WILLIAMS

DOUG AND JACK

My favorite memory from going to Hot Doug's was talking to Doug at the counter while my wife and I were on our way to a Blackhawks game. We asked Doug if he was going to watch the game, to which he responded: "Yes, I'll be watching the game with my friend Jack...Jack Daniel's." Classic. —**JUSTIN BREEN**

"IT WAS THE BEST OF TIMES, IT WAS THE WORST OF TIMES."

Those words, from Charles Dickens's *A Tale of Two Cities*, describe my life when I started regularly eating at Hot Doug's in the fall of 2006. I was doing my student teaching and was feeling all the excitement and anticipation of transitioning from college student to adult. It was the best of times.

However, parts of my teaching experience left much to be desired. The job was difficult and I never found my place in the teacher's lounge. It quickly reached a point when I simply avoided that room and took walks alone instead. It was the worst of times.

I began making it a normal habit to stop by Hot Doug's after school several days a week to make up for the lunch that I had opted to skip during the day. But it quickly became a much more important place for me—a place where I felt accepted and known. It was little things: Doug's warm conversation, how quickly Doug learned my name and order, the orange sugar cookies that he gave out for Halloween that year.

But one moment in particular stands out. I was having a bad day at school. And it was raining, making my bicycle commute much less enjoyable. After my last class, I made the quick bike ride over, locked up, and stood in line. I was tired, frustrated, and wet. I placed my order, reached into my wallet, and discovered it was empty. I thought, "How could this day get worse?!" I explained my situation and turned toward the door to head home without a hot dog. Then Doug very casually said, "Don't worry about it, you can pay next time," and filed my order card next to the register. Noticing my shock, he motioned me toward the drinks and said again, "Don't worry about it. I know you. You're good for it."

That moment changed my day and made me a Hot Doug's fan for life. This story illustrates Doug's generosity, trust, and care. On a basic level, I was having a bad day and Doug made it a whole lot better. On a deeper level, during a time when I felt anonymous, unknown, and unwanted, I felt the opposite way at Hot Doug's. I came back promptly the next day to repay what I owed for the hot dog, but I still feel indebted to him for his kindness to me in that season of life. I'm no longer a teacher—thank goodness!—but I still eat at Hot Doug's as often as I can.

—**ANDY MEYER**

THE GREAT AND POWERFUL HOT DOG

My favorite story is when a couple of kids, about five or six years old, were looking at all the items in the display case. They looked up at Doug, he smiled and said, "I am the great and powerful Oz." They looked at each other a little puzzled. Then they smiled and the girl looked back said, "No you are not, you are hot dog."

—**PHIL G.**

217

DOUGLAS SOUL

The end of the school year was fast approaching when I happened upon the student roster for the start of seventh grade on the principal's desk. I glanced over the names and noticed a new student set to arrive in the fall, a certain Douglas Soul. With a last name like that (it was at the height of soul music in the 1970s), I knew I had to meet this dude come fall. Obviously it was a typo (or more likely I misread it) but Douglas Soul turned out to be Douglas Sohn, who is now known to so many as Hot Doug.

Even though his last name wasn't Soul, Doug has always been one to put so much soul into whatever he attempts. I don't think I know of anyone who works as hard as Doug does and does so with such tremendous integrity. While waiting in line, it is a time to enjoy the wonderful camaraderie with fellow soon-to-be diners. Sitting close to the register, it is a time to eavesdrop on the always entertaining chatter with Doug and his customers. He takes great care and attention to every detail, from his hilarious menu, to the restaurant's outrageously fun decor, to the delicious culinary options he offers, and of course, the time he takes to make each person who crosses his path be entertained, feel special, and become enamored with this truly extraordinary individual.

DON ROSS IS MY OLDEST, DEAREST FRIEND AND LIVES IN SAN DIEGO—A TOWN WITH GENUINELY BAD HOT DOGS. HE, TOO, IS VERY PRETTY.

His creativity with food, creativity with words, written and spoken, are really second to none. His food is unbelievably delicious. What makes Hot Doug's and Doug so special is Doug. He takes unfathomable care to provide a unique and positive experience for his customers. He lives by the credo, "Treat others as you would like them to treat you."

Hot Doug's is a testament of who Doug is. He is someone who cares deeply about his customers, his staff, and his purveyors. The grand smiles on peoples' faces after talking with Doug and dining on his offerings are a testament to what is truly a memorable, fine dining experience. It is what a great restaurant should be. And I don't think you can find a much better man out there, or a better friend, than Doug is. You're so pretty! **—DON ROSS**

TOUGH LOVE

I have been going to Hot Doug's for a few years now, but my real connection to Hot Doug's began in 2011. I finally moved to Chicago after years of wishing and not acting. Naturally, Doug's became a weekly pilgrimage. Doug came to know my name after a month or so, and the conversation really started to pick (and heat) up. I soon learned of Doug's affinity for 1970s Roller Derby (see: The Dave Pound), Elle "The Body" Macpherson, and Gisele Bündchen. Back to ME though.

I was having trouble finding a decent job, and decided to take the easy way out and move back home. I informed Doug that my weekly trips would end, and my life as I knew it was going in reverse. He asked where home was. I told him "a small town in central Illinois, three hours south of here." He then insisted, "Yeah, where?" I said "Charleston, Illinois. It's 45 minutes south of Champaign." He responded with, "Well, that's unfortunate news for anybody." I laughed and completely agreed.

The day I was supposed to move back I woke up, started dry heaving, and realized the huge mistake I was about to make (no more Hot Doug's, Belmont Barbershop, friends, urine smell of the CTA). I quickly changed my mind and stayed. The following week I received two job offers and finally secured a halfway acceptable form of employment. When I told Doug I was staying, he graciously mumbled that I was a "mother*&^#$" and that he practices a "tough kind of love." Then he spotted me lunch. If Chicago has a man like Doug Sohn it will always be a world-class place in my book. Doug is lovingly snarky, and a truly sharp, generous, kind, and thoughtful person. Hot Doug's is a testament to that. **—RHETT HITE**

GO TEAM FOOD&LIQUOR

Hot Doug's sponsored our local ultimate frisbee club team, Food&Liquor, in 2008. When we claimed this Chicago name for ourselves, we were very picky about the Chicago food we would associate the team with. It was an honor to have the chance to honor Hot Dougs. We were not at all picky about the liquor. —GALEN GRAHAM

Food and Liquor ultimate frisbee team: Top photo: Matt Snoap; bottom photo: Pepe Peplinski, Liz Langer, Peter Behr, Galen Graham, Deepak Kulkarni, Taylor Dall, and Jorge Duarte.

Dougouts Team Photo from 2012, back row: Omar Diaz, Phil Paris, Andrew Goldman, Justin Arrieta, Kate Alpert; middle row: Anne Benjamin, Kim Richards, Linda Enzbiglis; front row: Robert Nikolov, Dmitry Shub, Adam Andersen, Therese Stanko.

THE HOT DOUG'S DOUGOUTS

For the past few years, Doug has been generous enough to support our 16-inch softball co-ed recreational team: The Hot Doug's Dougouts. After many seasons of "Cubs-like" performance, in 2012 we won our bracket's summer championship. People always tell us how much they love Hot Doug's and ask if we work there. We don't—we're just fans and our sponsorship came about because we play at the field Brands Park right behind the restaurant. We can understand the confusion: our chant after games when we all put our hands in a circle is "Duck Fat Fries."

The logo was designed by Billy Baumann, who is also our right-fielder. We made Doug an honorary #1 jersey, and we also made him a card for being our sponsor. —KATE ALPERT

POSTSCRIPT:

Three Last Things...

Top 11 Rejected Book titles:

1. Who Moved my Cheese Fries
2. 50 Shades of Mustard
3. Wiener Confidential
4. The Da Vinci Code
5. Are You There Madonna? It's me, Doug
6. What the Foie Are You Lookin' At
7. Dog Day Afternoon
8. Bshert: The Blessed life of a Swinging Gentile
9. Masterpâté
10. Hunger Games
11. The Poky Little Doggy

For those of you who thought this was going to be a cookbook

The first time I was asked to do a book, the proposal was an actual cookbook. It turns out, it's really hard to sell a seven-page cookbook.

But I'd feel remiss if I didn't include at least one recipe, so here goes.

HOT DOG

SERVES: 1

INGREDIENTS:

1 hot dog
1 bun
Condiments

METHOD:

Cook hot dog until done. Place in bun. Put condiments on top. Serve with french fries or side salad. (I'm kidding about the side salad.)

PHOTO OPPOSITE PAGE BY CHRIS MARKOS

Acknowledgments

Since my publisher said I couldn't make the book 400 pages long (paper costs or some such nonsense), I am obligated to limit my thank-yous. So, if I've forgotten you, I do apologize and promise to buy you a hot dog the next time you come in.

First of all, thank you to my family. Dad (he named it, after all), mom, my brother Andy who drove around with me looking for spaces and offered solid business advice, and my nephews Charlie and James—the two biggest hot dogs I know.

Thank you to everyone who helped me get this shindig off the ground: the Hot Dog Club, including Paul Kelly, Leah Yarrow, and junior member Jill Oldham; all of you who helped paint and clean; Judine O'Shea and Carrie Gowran for the great logo; Nick Markos for the catchiest restaurant theme song ever; Arthur Ellis for his legal expertise and saving me a boatload of money (and not just by working for hot dogs); Jim Scherzinger and Karen Snodgrass for helping me fill out the forms I have no patience for; Robert Truska for making sure I don't go homeless if there's ever, God forbid, a fire or flood (um, wait a second...); Gary Manning for being kind enough to be my first (and, for awhile, only) employee; and pizza-maker extraordinaire Mark Bello for his ingenuity and incredible design work.

Thank you to a great group of purveyors and sales reps who provide the stuff I try very hard not to screw up: everyone at Vienna Beef, including my first salesman John Alexakos who, rumor has it, gave me six months (I would've said the same); the wonderful Deb "Cookie" Einhorn at European Imports (and formerly of Tonelli's Pizza, which was near and dear to my heart); George at Columbus Meats; Lizet at Sysco; Jim at Chicago Game; Kris at Artisan; Mark at Paulina Meat Market; Joelle at D'Artagnan; Paul, Kyle, and Cosmo at Publican Quality Meats; and everyone around the world making great sausage for us.

A very special thank you to Michael Helminiak of MGH Foods. Not only is he the greatest purveyor/sales rep/customer service guy anywhere to be found, but I'm honored that we've become good friends.

Thank you to the Lane Tech kids who basically kept me in business the first two years.

Thank you to Paul "Small Fry" Brinkmann, Greg Susinka, and Rick "The Rabbi" Gorgoni for keeping the restaurant functioning and in one piece; Louise Ahrendt for spiffing up the place and letting me pretend to be a Medici; Mitch and Scott Silver at Printable Promotions for the t-shirts, hats, and generous discounts; and Rick Linus and Benchmark for more t-shirts and great designs.

Thank you to Brendan Fitzpatrick for taking it upon himself, unbeknownst to me, to be the Hot Doug's Social Media Director (now there's resume material!); and Matt Green for his very persuasive argument and helping to convince me to do this book.

Thank you to everyone at Agate Publishing for pitching and taking on this project: Doug Seibold, Danielle McLimore, Jennifer Sikora, Anjali Becker, Zach Rudin, and Eileen Johnson; and Al Brandtner for a knockout design—when I told him I wanted the book to look like the restaurant, he obviously understood what I was saying.

Thank you to the photographers and illustrators: Roya Jade, Ian Merritt, Johnny Villalobos, Chris Markos, and Chris Posdal. Your wonderful images not only make the book look great, but created less space for me to have to fill in.

Thank you to every customer who contributed to this book and to everyone who has waited in line, bought a sausage, and kept me from having to look for a different job.

Thank you to the greatest restaurant staff on the planet: Octavio, Carlos, Lalo, Benjamin, Justin, Kristina, Marco, Michael, Anthony, and Georgia. My job is so much easier because of you.

I can't begin to express my truly heartfelt thanks to Kate DeVivo for her extraordinary dedication and work on this book. Smart, funny, and a genuinely talented writer and editor, I do not envy her task of keeping me organized and on point. I would be honored if she were to allow me to work with her again. This book wouldn't have happened without her. She's also easy on the eyes.